The Life That Changed My Day

The Life That Changed My Day

Authentic

First published in 2004 by Authentic Lifestyle

10 09 08 07 06 05 04   7 6 5 4 3 2
Reprinted 2004 by Authentic Media
9 Holdom Avenue, Bletchley, Milton Keynes, Bucks., MK1 1QR
and PO Box 1047, Waynesboro, GA 30830-2047, USA
www.authenticmedia.co.uk

British Library Cataloguing in Publication Data

A catalogue record for this book is available from the Briitsh Library

ISBN 1-85078-549-X

Cover design by David Lund
Printed in Denmark by
Norhaven

Contents

Foreword ix

1 Choose Your Rut Carefully 1

2 Glimpses of God 9

3 Who Do You Think You Are? 23

4 Prisoner of the Past 34

5 Living in the Waiting Room 50

6 Will Jesus Step Out of the Sky One Day? 64

7 Up Close and Personal 82

8 Our Father 103

9 Facing the Truth 120

10 Open Your Eyes and Look! 133

11 Set Off and See! 155

Notes 172

To the man I love and the children we love. Thank you for seeing life as an adventure and for embracing all those who you meet along the way.

Foreword

Read this book! A friend of mine who is a friend of the God who can be a friend to you writes it! It is practical, honest, funny, and whimsical. It has a habit of sneaking up on you; getting your soul by the scruff of its neck and making it turn its distracted thoughts God ward.

Read this book! You need to read this book! Somehow – with the help of God of course – Hilary Price takes us with her down a personal path that leads inexorably to the God she loves to distraction, the Christ she serves with exuberance, and the Holy Spirit who inspires her to capture that journey on paper so we can savour it all.

Read this book! You need to read this book because all of us have a heart hunger and a spiritual thirst that, like the woman at the well, can alone be met by a living dynamic Christ who invites us to take our fill of Him.

Let Hilary open the life of a woman to you, who thousands of years ago stumbled towards a well of hope through the middle Eastern heat, and found her withered soul revelling in the refreshing of God. Can such a meeting of this same God and little people like you and me happen to day? Oh yes—read this book!

Hilary weaves such bright truth into her story, it lights up the way to deal with a past that need forgiveness, a future that needs to be secured, and a present that for too many people can only be described as a rut (a grave with the ends knocked out!).

From her vantage point of motherhood, missionary ministry, and the many challenges of marriage to a prominent preacher, Hilary pushes us beyond the surface of our shallow faith concepts to think through the dynamics of how it all works. This Christianity that some say can never be boring (yet many of us secretly admit is) walks off these pages into our lives to settle down and instruct us in the way of Life that works. How can disappointments, death, divorce and depression be keys to unlock the mercies of god and make them real and relevant to our dilemmas? Read this book!

It's not easy to open your life to the world and invite its scrutiny. There is an old English saying that opines, 'He that raiseth his or her head above the crowd inviteth a tomatoe!' I have found that old adage to be true! You only take that risk if you have found comfort in the God of all comfort, who expects you then to get out and about comforting others with the comfort you have received of Him.

Hilary has had her share of human pain, She has found a way to use it to drive her deeper into God, and has a deep desire to show others how it works. That's another good reason to 'read this book' All of us need to know how to do that! Happy reading.

Jill Briscoe

Chapter 1

Choose Your Rut Carefully

What would you say has been the most important day of your life? Obviously the day you were born was important, but what about the days since then? Does any one stand out as being a day on which everything else has hinged?

A day can be important in itself, like your first day at school or the day your first child was born, or it may seem very ordinary until something happens which changes the rest of your life: a phone call, an accident, a chance conversation, a letter, a doctor's appointment.

Maybe you are still waiting for that defining moment, that special day. Maybe life is made up of seamless days of meaninglessness, punctuated only by trips to the supermarket where you will buy exactly what you bought last week!

When you were little and you dreamed of what you would do when you grew up, was it what you are actually doing now? Look at your day, the one you have just had or the one that lies ahead, is this how you envisaged it would all work out? You may be tired simply because you feel old and unstimulated, or you could be exhausted through overwork. You may be frazzled after a busy day in the office, disappointed because yet another relationship has come to an end, hassled after a fraught journey on the train, excited because the kids at school, where you teach, really got into the lesson you sat up preparing late last night, anxious because your teenager slammed the door as she left this morning and you were sure you heard her muttering a word you didn't even think she knew!

Are you married and wish you weren't? Unmarried and wish you were? Unemployed and defeated by the sense of worthlessness that each empty day brings? Overloaded in a job which demands more hours than you can give and pays no more however much you give? Longing for children? Overwhelmed by the stress of bringing up three pre-schoolers on your own? Looking back from the perspective of retirement and wondering where all those years have gone? How about where you actually live? Is it what you dreamed it would be, that trendy flat in the city in the midst of all the hustle and bustle, that little cottage in the country, with the white picket fence and chickens in the yard, where you are away from it all and free to be you?

I have been told that just as you enter the desert, at a certain point in the Australian outback, a sign has been strategically placed with this warning, CHOOSE YOUR RUT CAREFULLY – YOU'LL BE IN IT FOR THE NEXT 500 MILES. If that sign was erected on the path along which you now find yourself travelling, I wonder if you would be excited and keen to keep going just as you are, or so terrified at the prospect, that you would stop in your tracks and look for the nearest exit.

Some people feel incredibly stuck in their lives and they are not sure how they got there. I recently heard a woman on the television saying, 'I feel too young to be old and too old to be young.' With two teenage daughters, I sympathise. If I appear in clothes that are too trendy they say, 'Mum!' – giving the word far more syllables than it usually has – and then ask, 'Is that jacket new?' I get the message. There is no going back, I can only go forward and I am certainly not ready to join in with the 'Well it's downhill all the way now' mentality. Most of us still believe we are heading for the summit, however old we may be, and deep down we never want to get there.

One of my friends was venting her frustration with life down the phone at me the other day as she wrestled with this feeling of treading water. 'If I don't do something soon,' she wailed, 'I shall be living like this for the rest of my life – cooking, cleaning, shopping, tidying – in the house all my life, just like my mum.'

If we were honest, most of us would have to admit that we didn't choose our rut very carefully and now we've been in it so long, it is almost impossible to think that there may be an alternative. We may have become comfortable, but we are not content. Take a deep breath and look at your rut. 'How will I know when I am in a rut?' you might be asking. You'll know when there is a nagging little voice constantly whispering in your ear, 'There must be more to life than this,' but you haven't the imagination, the inclination or the energy to do anything about it. So how are you coping, what strategies do you find yourself adopting to pretend to yourself, and the public at large, that life in the rut is really meaningful?

Perhaps you stay just as you are but become busier and busier to convince yourself that your rut is a wonderful place to be. As you run faster and faster, backwards and forwards, like a little mole digging a tunnel, it will gradually become deeper and darker, so you can do the next thing, you can distract yourself from the emptiness of it all and brighten up your rut. You can redecorate faster than you can say 'Changing Rooms' and, wonder of wonders, there is a weekly TV programme for people just like you. New bedroom, new curtains, transform your garden to look like an Italian courtyard in a weekend and not only will you enjoy your rut so much more, but you can invite your neighbours over for a barbecue on all those warm summer evenings and they can escape their rut momentarily and enjoy it too!

And if you have them, children can make life so worthwhile. Undoubtedly, family life is fulfilling. But, beware – children can allow you to fill a void when you live out your unfulfilled longings through them. Drive them to gymnastics, football trials, tennis coaching, drama auditions, and give them the opportunity not only to do all the things you always wanted to do, but to be the best at it. Their achievements bring a wonderful sense of pride. You praise and encourage them, but ironically your personal frustrations are compounded and your willingness to sit in draughty corridors outside practice rooms and drive miles every Saturday to those all-important competitions can very slowly and silently turn to an obsessive competitiveness. The fun has gone, you are driving them to their limits and even if they reach a point where they want to quit, you don't. You have invested all this time and money in them and are determined they will have something to show for it all.

Another very different way of making life in your rut more bearable is not to get on the treadmill of activity at all, but to become completely passive. In fact you can sit down in your favourite comfy chair to do this one while regularly peeping into other people's ruts to see how they live. Of course not literally over the garden fence, that would be far too obvious, but through soap operas, salacious articles in the tabloids and if you're very daring, by anonymously venturing into chat rooms on the internet to 'visit' other faceless, anonymous, lonely people. The Beatles used to question in one of their songs, 'All those lonely people, where do they all come from? All those lonely people, where do they all belong?' Well now they have found somewhere to belong. No commitments, no strings attached, but a wonderful chance to escape the rut with the thrill of going online.

We have become an incredibly voyeuristic society. We want to know the intimate and exciting lifestyle details of all the stars, the royal family, and the politicians. Our ruts may have become dull and boring, but theirs look so exciting and we know we can get a vicarious thrill through watching what they do, what they wear and where they go. How sad to conclude I can never be that or do that, but never mind, I can watch someone else do it from the comfort of my armchair. How sad to realise that the fantasy relationships between the people on the television have become more important than the real relationships in which I am involved. In fact you didn't invite your neighbour in when she called round last night because you'd just got to an exiting moment in *Knocksville*, or whatever it is you watch on Tuesdays and Thursdays, and Des was just about to walk in on Samantha who was having an affair with Steve and if you stood there talking to Mrs Jones from next door, who does tend to go on a bit, you'd miss it all. You've been waiting for Samantha to get her comeuppance for three weeks since she lied to Clare because you like Clare, she's so pretty . . .

The only difference between a rut and a grave is that the grave has the ends blocked in.

How many of us actually do what we want to do, become who we hoped we'd be and live where we feel we belong? Over the past few years I have spent a lot of time with my father. He and my mother are divorced. He is a retired headmaster and French teacher and recently he has completely lost his hearing. We have made numerous trips to the hospital in Manchester, in the North of England, and it was on one of these trips that I saw how his life, like most of ours if we were honest, still contained unfulfilled longings. As we waited at a set of traffic lights, he pointed out a street where he used to walk during his lunch break from his job at a bank. He always used to eat his sandwich outside the office of a shipping company, gazing in the window at a model liner and dreaming of the day he would become a ship's captain. He never became a ship's captain. Instead, he joined the navy when the Second World War broke out and went to sea, with thousands of other eager young men, in a corvette.

When my dad left the navy, he left his dream behind and put plan 'B' into operation: he trained and became a teacher; it was the sensible and practical thing to do. Marriage and two children followed and after almost twenty-four years, when both of us girls had left home, came divorce. Since he went deaf I have listened to my father more than ever before, and I am privileged to have been entrusted with more of his inner thoughts than ever before. One of the saddest things he said to me, about a year ago, was when he was explaining how as he gets older things from the distant past become far more vivid and real than recent happenings. As with many of us his dreams at night allow him to revisit places no longer accessible to him. After a particularly intense dream he simply said, 'In my dreams we are still a family.' These aren't dreams that look forward with hope and anticipation, but dreams that look back with longing and regret and a realisation that now they can never be.

Are your dreams wistful or hopeful? Are you trying to make them work or being forced to let them go? Has one particular day brought them all crashing down or are you still waiting for that one special day and moment which will turn them into reality?

One of my favourite people in the Bible is someone who is given no name; she is described simply as 'a woman'. To me she represents every human being who goes about their daily tasks with a deep sense of longing. Her dreams have died and with nothing to replace them, she doggedly does what she has to do, trudging up and down her well-worn rut, numb with disappointment, clutching a threadbare shawl of dignity around her to protect herself against a society where she has become an outcast.

Every day she sets off to draw water from the well. She drops the bucket down empty and pulls the bucket up full, fresh and sparkling. As she pours the water into her stone jar, before heaving it onto her shoulder for the long walk home, she laughs to herself, 'So much water and yet such a thirst. Deep down I have such a thirst for real love and real purpose and no one knows.' She has gone through this mindless routine for years, she has no choice and sadly she no longer has any expectation that things will ever be different. But one day . . .

Jesus . . . had to go through Samaria. So he came to a town in Samaria called Sychar, near the plot of ground Jacob had given to his son Joseph. Jacob's well was there, and Jesus, tired as he was from the journey, sat down by the well. It was about the sixth hour.

When a Samaritan woman came to draw water, Jesus said to her, 'Will you give me a drink?' (His disciples had gone into the town to buy food.)

The Samaritan woman said to him, 'You are a Jew and I am a Samaritan woman. How can you ask me for a drink?' (For Jews do not associate with Samaritans.)

Jesus answered her, 'If you knew the gift of God and who it is that asks you for a drink, you would have asked him and he would have given you living water.'

'Sir,' the woman said, 'you have nothing to draw with and the well is deep. Where can you get this living water? Are you greater than our father Jacob, who gave us the well and drank from it himself, as did also his sons and his flocks and herds?'

Jesus answered, 'Everyone who drinks this water will be thirsty again, but whoever drinks the water I give him will never thirst. Indeed the water I give him will become in him a spring of water welling up to eternal life.'

The woman said to him, 'Sir give me this water so that I won't get thirsty and have to keep coming here to draw water.'

He told her, 'Go call your husband and come back.'

'I have no husband,' she replied.

Jesus said to her, 'You are right when you say you have no husband. The fact is, you have had five husbands, and the man you now have is not your husband. What you have just said is quite true.'

'Sir,' the woman said, 'I can see that you are a prophet. Our fathers worshipped on this mountain, but you Jews claim that the place where we must worship is in Jerusalem.'

Jesus declared, 'Believe me, woman, a time is coming when you will worship the Father neither on this mountain nor in Jerusalem. You Samaritans worship what you do not know, we worship what we do know, for salvation is from the Jews. Yet a time is coming and has now come when the true worshippers will worship the Father in spirit and truth, for they are the kind of worshippers the

Father seeks. God is spirit, and his worshippers must worship in spirit and in truth.'

The woman said, 'I know that Messiah' (called Christ) 'is coming. When he comes, he will explain everything to us.'

Then Jesus declared, 'I who speak to you am he.'

Just then the disciples returned and were surprised to find him talking with a woman. But no-one asked, 'What do you want?' or 'Why are you talking with her?'

Then, leaving her water jar, the woman went back to the town and said to the people, 'Come, see a man who told me everything I ever did. Could this be the Christ?' They came out of the town and made their way towards him.

Meanwhile his disciples urged him, 'Rabbi, eat something.'

But he said to them, 'I have food to eat that you know nothing about.'

Then his disciples said to each other, 'Could someone have brought him food?'

'My food,' said Jesus, 'is to do the will of him who sent me and to finish his work. Do you not say, "Four months more and then the harvest"? I tell you, open your eyes and look at the fields! They are ripe for harvest. Even now the reaper draws his wages, even now he harvests the crop for eternal life, so that the sower and the reaper may be glad together. Thus the saying, "One sows and another reaps" is true. I sent you to reap what you have not worked for. Others have done the hard work, and you have reaped the benefits of their labour.'

Many of the Samaritans from that town believed in him because of the woman's testimony, 'He told me everything I ever did.' So when the Samaritans came to him, they urged him to stay with them, and he stayed two days. And because of his words many more became believers.

They said to the woman, 'We no longer believe just because of what you said; now we have heard for ourselves, and we know this man really is the Saviour of the world' (Jn. 4:4–42).

Chapter 2

Glimpses of God

'If you knew the gift of God . . .'

The morning had started like any other morning. The woman had stirred as she heard the soft thud of the door shutting. She stretched her foot across the mattress and knew she was alone. The man always left as the sun came up. He would be away all day, working in the fields and tonight they would reunite. He would be tired from the day's labour; she would be tired from the day's routine. Early morning had always been her favourite time of the day. She used to love setting off, while the world was still cool, with her water jar on her shoulder and her mind full of the chatter she would share with her friends as they gathered around the well.

But times changed when she became the main source of all the gossip. Men had come and gone. They had promised much but delivered so little. Marriage now seemed a worthless ritual. It brought no guarantees and she was no longer willing to hide behind its façade. The local women frowned on her. It was not acceptable to have been through so many divorces, and to simply live with someone was beneath contempt. They never talked to her about it; they just one by one made their judgement and kept their distance.

She did what she did out of a sense of true integrity to herself. She hated hypocrisy and she was not willing to pretend any longer. She had tried to hold her head high and walk among them as usual, but as time went on it became easier to simply withdraw and make her journey alone, to the well furthest from the town, in the heat of the day, knowing there would never be anyone there to sneer at her or snub her with their averted eyes and turned backs.

She stretched, wondering whether to go back to sleep or to get up and begin the day's chores. There was always sweeping and cleaning to do, bread to bake, clothes to wash and a trip to the market to be made before any of the other women returned from the well. Today she felt tired in a weary sort of way. There was enough bread left to last from yesterday, the man never seemed to notice whether she cleaned or not and maybe she could get the leftovers from the market stalls when the shoppers had gone home and the merchants began to close down at the end of the day. She would sleep.

When she woke again it was with a sudden jerk. The noonday sun was blazing in at the small window on her face and as everyone else retired for their siesta, she knew it was time to make her daily journey to get water. She dragged her body from the mattress, with that leaden feeling that comes from sleeping late into the morning, and went to get a quick drink. The jar was empty and she has no choice but to hoist it onto her shoulder and set off with a dry throat and parched lips.

As she emerged from her small dwelling she automatically shaded her eyes from the sun in the blinding heat of the day. Her body was stooped and her feet dragged; she regretted her morning's slumber. It was always so tempting to slip away into sleep. It was a wonderful escape. But everything seemed so much heavier when it was time to re-emerge and face the world again.

The woman's eyes were fixed on the stony ground as she approached the well. She was shocked when she raised her head to find someone sitting right where she usually rested her jar. She hesitated. Her shoulder was hurting and she wanted to be free of the weight, but she was caught in a moment of indecision. Should she turn around and go back? Should she carry on with the process of taking off the wooden cover and lowering the bucket and just pretend she hadn't seen him. That was not possible, she would have to pass him to reach the bucket. Should she . . . She was trying to think of a third option, when to her amazement and relief the man spoke. He was asking her a question and she was so surprised that she found herself lowering her jar and starting to answer.

The conversation that he struck up with her was truly remarkable. It probably only took about thirty minutes and yet it covered her whole life: her past, her present and her future. She arrived at the familiar spot alone and unknown; she left aware she was completely known, probably for the first time in her life. Instead of being frightened by the exposure, she was freed by it. She may have arrived with her head bowed, but she certainly left with it held high; as she retraced her steps to the town, she knew she had been changed.

In this book I want to look at what happened at their meeting, drawing out principles which apply to each of us, while at the same time retracing my own steps, which also led to a personal encounter with the one who knows me better than I know myself. His probing questions and penetrating eyes are not to be feared because they belong to the one whose sole motivation for drawing near is to love and invite each one of us to come back to where we really belong, however far we may have wandered.

The woman did not expect to find anyone sitting on the well. She certainly did not expect to find God sitting on the well any more than we would expect to find him standing by the shopping trolleys outside the supermarket! Her ideas about God had never been really formulated. Like many of us they were vague, sort of inherited from those around her, but with a little probing proved to be unsatisfactory and impersonal. 'You worship what you do not know,' Jesus told her. That statement was not only true about her but was also an incredibly apt description of humanity today in the twenty-first century.

In the United Kingdom, where I have lived most of my life, well over half the population believe in God. But what do they believe and where did they get their ideas from? I want, at this point to tell you how I fumbled my way towards God, not because I think I am special in any way, but on the contrary because I think my journey is fairly typical and my glimpses of God are easily recognisable. So many of us pick up the clues, but we fail to find the treasure. Years ago I wrote a poem, which opened with these lines,

> As you wander by the seashore of your mind
> Picking up the pieces you can find
> Have you ever formed a picture?

This is how my picture of God gradually began to emerge. I believe all of us have pieces from the 'I wonder if there is a God and what he is like' jigsaw, all jumbled up in a box somewhere in our minds. In our family we don't do jigsaws unless we are ill! Or should I say, when we've been ill and forced to convalesce, find we have time on our hands. It takes time to put the pieces together, work out what you believe and where you have maybe unknowingly glimpsed God. Most of us don't have the chance of thirty minutes, face to face with Jesus, to guide us in our thoughts, but simply finding the thirty minutes to be alone to think would be a good start! That's about how long it took me, jotting notes at great speed on a large piece of paper, to look back over forty-six years asking God, 'Where were you God?' and concluding . . . well I'll save that until I get to the conclusion!

I didn't grow up believing in God, I didn't grow up not believing in him, I just grew up with a vague idea that earth hung in a very big space and there must be something out there. That kind of thinking caused me problems because I wanted to reach the 'end' and feel secure in a kind of closed universe. When I tried to think about God my mind always fell off the edge and because I couldn't see what was there I retreated. When I was about six years old I lingered at the back of the church, which we visited occasionally and always at Christmas and Easter, to ask what I thought would be the definitive question. If I got an answer to this, then I could begin to feel comfortable in this world and not have to keep 'falling off the edge'. Finally the vicar was alone and I blurted it out: 'If God made the world, who made God?' He didn't answer my question. He patted me on the head and said, 'Now run along little girl, you shouldn't be bothering your head with things like that.' I wasn't taken in. I realised that he did not know the answer! Instead of leaving, feeling safer than ever, I left feeling very insecure deep down and with the seeds of cynicism about Anglican vicars who worked for a God they didn't even know, well and truly planted in my heart!

I know I was very young, but there were things I wanted to sort out and they churned away inside me. After the failure to get anywhere with the vicar, I tried to explore my own thoughts and logic, but found myself going round and round in circles. The other area of concern in my world was prompted by simply opening my eyes. I instinctively believed in heaven, not because anyone taught me about it, but because I loved the sky. I would often lie on my back in the summer and gaze above me. All I could see was a blue sky and the more I looked the more I felt as though I was being physically drawn towards it. It almost seemed as though I had to lie heavily on the earth so I wouldn't get sucked in. Something in me wanted to be drawn upwards, but again I was scared of falling off the edge. What was up there, beyond the beyond? Since I could not find out without actually going there, the next obvious question began to formulate in my mind: was there anyone who had been to heaven and then come back to earth? If there was, then they could tell us all about it and put my mind at rest. I didn't try the vicar this time, I tried my sister, who was three years older than me and therefore I was sure knew much more than I did: she didn't seem to think anyone had completed this journey. I was disappointed but realised it was a bit of a fantastical idea anyway.

Although I never pursued that line of questioning on heaven again, the implications of not having reached a satisfactory answer never left me. Well into my teens, I would lie awake at night, on my own, saying over and over again in my head, 'One day I am going to die.' I wanted to stop the thought and somehow expel it from my head, but it would circle round and round, tormenting me and eventually shouting at me with an urgency I could not stand. I would have to get out of the bed and go to the bathroom to wipe my now sweaty, clammy forehead. I would only get to sleep by reading a nice kind of book, which made me feel comfortable and safe and gradually allowed me to escape the spiral, which I knew I would find myself spinning down again sooner or later.

As I said, we sometimes went to church but I have no memory of anything that went on there ever being explained. We did not talk about God in everyday conversation in our home. I knew Granny believed in him completely, I presumed my mother and father did. But I knew my sister did not really believe at all, despite her willingness to go to confirmation classes and be presented with a pink shiny prayer book for her troubles. I did not see the point. Nothing in the church seemed real to me. It was a tall stone, towering building where people spoke in hushed voices, sang songs they appeared to make up as they went along and expected us to sit still for what seemed like a very long time with nothing to do except gaze at all the colours and shapes in the stained glass windows. I had lots of questions about the beginning of the world, heaven and death, and nothing in the church gave me any answers. There was no Sunday school and children were invisible until they fidgeted. I concluded that you had to be grown up and preferably very old, like Granny to get on with God and since I was very young and I didn't want to get confirmed, I decided that to be true to myself, the best thing I could do, was to call it a day and never go to church again unless I really had to with the guides and the school and on other boring, formal occasions.

I stuck to my decision until I was about fourteen years old, when for some reason I decided to go to church with a friend of mine every other weekend for a year. As soon as the year was over, I quit. All my worst feelings about the whole church environment had only been compounded. Now I was a teenager I had started looking for love in relationships, which in time would soon lead to a lot of hurt and confusion; in that whole year, no one in the church ever told me God loved me in a language that connected with a teenager. It is no good saying, 'If only they had.' As far as I was concerned I had given God another go. I had visited what people called his house and he had not turned up. I did not know it was possible to find God anywhere other than in the church, so I was forced to reach the rather frightening conclusion that he did not exist.

I still had my nagging worries about the blue abyss above and the terror of dying and falling off the edge, but I managed to submerge them in the busyness of being a teenager. There were two Christians in my class at high school, but they were not in my social group and I was too 'cool' to ever even talk to them! I never even admitted to my friends that I had such dark thoughts about death that sometimes I couldn't sleep at night, so I certainly would never have admitted it to them, or asked them for answers to some of the questions that troubled me. Anyway now other things had become more important. There were boys to flirt with, a world of sport to throw myself into and lessons and homework to fill my mind. I no longer gave God any time or thought, I simply got caught up in the whirlwind of living in the present and making the best of now, since that was all there was I could be sure of.

For me, religion and church had put up barriers around any God who may have been there. Rather than revealing him to me they had obscured if not obliterated him. Nevertheless, I did have glimpses of God, outside the confines of the church, which were completely spontaneous and so real that I have never forgotten them. They impacted my mind as light impacts a film when the shutter opens even for a split second. The image they left had captured a moment in time and it is still as vivid to me as it was on the day it happened.

My first glimpse of God was not to do with him as a being or as a defined person, but simply to do with vastness and mystery. I was about ten and was playing in the back garden with my friend. We were taking turns on the swing. One of us sat on the cross bar while the other one swung. When it came to my turn on the swing I lent backwards to see the sky lurching backwards and forwards way up above me. To my amazement I realised the clouds had formed a pattern that looked like a vast fence or a series of gates. I remember gasping and thinking, 'That must be the gates of heaven. God must be there, just on the other side.' I wasn't frightened, I was very excited and a shiver ran through my body. I didn't want to tell my friend because I felt as though it was a private and very personal message, a sign just for me. She must have seen me staring and she started to look up. 'Look,' I said, 'Can you see the gates of heaven, there in the sky?' 'Don't be so daft,' she said, 'it's just clouds.' But I had seen something else and I was sure God was there in the vast blue unknown, and he was watching. We were two young girls in a tiny back garden in Yorkshire, but he was watching.

A few weeks later I did a simple experiment. I wanted to know whether if God was there, as I had sensed him to be in the sky, then was he everywhere? Could he always see everything I did? I sat on my bed in my bedroom longing to believe that there was someone who knew all about me. I had felt it in the garden. It had been wonderful, but was it real? I knew there was a deep-down me that nobody knew. There were thoughts and feelings I hid from my parents. I tried to write a diary several times between the ages of about eight and eleven, but I never got past the first few pages, because even at that young age I wrestled with things that disturbed me. I felt that the diary of a girl of that age should be all happy and record a life rather like that of the children in *The Famous Five*, a novel by the popular author, Enid Blyton, full of innocent adventures and fun. But my life wasn't like theirs and I felt ashamed that I felt what I now realise was depressed. I didn't know what to do with the blackness and I would never have had the confidence to write it all down and actually admit it to anyone. I just wished that someone knew. I simply sat there and clicked my fingers and thought, 'Is there anyone who can see me, who can see through doors and walls and knows that I just did that? It was very still and silent and I concluded that there was no one who saw. Much as I wanted there to be; I was on my own and I felt very lonely in a place within me that I didn't understand. I can see now that I was yearning for a sense of belonging, which I now know is so fundamental to every human being.

If each of us is handmade by God, then his stamp is on us even though we may not know it. However far we may wander in life, there will be times when we get that strange feeling that this is very familiar, I know this place or this emotion, at this moment I feel secure. It may not be the gates of heaven blazoned across the sky, it may simply be a glimpse of God's character in someone else who has been handmade by God and who knows where they belong. I had a teacher at high school, who did not know it then, and I am sure still does not know it, but whose courage and sheer goodness gave me glimpses of God which I was drawn to without understanding why. He was not my favourite teacher and he certainly did not teach my favourite subjects, he taught Religious Studies and Physics!

One day we were all sitting in one of his lessons, bored to tears, as we looked yet again at Paul's missionary journeys. They were of no interest to me, or as far as I could see anyone else in the class. Who was Paul anyway and why did all the maps with what looked like black snail trails all over them look the same? I wished he hadn't gone on so many journeys and they hadn't taken so long. We seemed to have been studying them for weeks. Suddenly I was roused from my stupor, a well-practised technique of looking vaguely interested while being miles away, by the teacher standing at the front of the class getting very animated and saying, 'I am a saint.' I think someone must have asked what a saint was and that was his reply. People started to snigger and he simply said it again, only this time he added, 'I am a saint – with a little 's'.' I had known he was a Christian, but here he was saying not only was he a saint, but all God's children were saints. The bell went, we were dismissed and we spent the rest of the day chanting his slogan, 'I am a saint – with a little 's' ' to all sorts of different, catchy tunes. I joined in, in fact I think I initiated the chanting accompanied by swinging body movements, but in that quiet place within I felt shame. I admired the man. I pretended I despised him, but I despised myself for pretending. He knew his God and he was not ashamed of it. He was small with glasses and slightly thinning hair and he had stood before us all, tall and radiant with the aura of God's pleasure around him. It was something I had never known and up to this point had not realised was possible. That mighty, mysterious being, who lived behind those huge cloud gates in the sky, had certain people on earth whom he was pleased with; how wonderful to be one of those people.

The next time this same teacher gave me a glimpse of his friend God, was during a registration period. He was our homeroom teacher and it was his responsibility to speak to us if any other teachers were concerned about our behaviour as a class. One of our teachers was in the early stages of having a nervous breakdown. I am sure that individually none of us would have hurt him, but as a class, we acted with a pack instinct joining in the process of humiliating him when we should have known better.

One day, when things had been particularly bad in our previous lesson, God's friend decided it was time to call us to account. He let us know that he was fully aware of what we were doing and then he simply asked, 'If you saw a man lying on the ground with a broken leg, would you kick him as you walked past?' I felt so ashamed. I knew I had not thrown icing sugar all over his back or put a drawing pin on his chair or been insolent when answering his questions, but I had enjoyed watching him squirm when other people played such pranks. He never saw them coming and I waited with gleeful anticipation for the inevitable red-faced, stuttering outburst. There is a wonderful moment in Jane Austen's *Emma*, when Emma has been particularly mean to her best friend and she is rebuked by the man who loves her and knows her behaviour has been well beneath her. 'Badly done Emma,' he says, 'badly done.' Through this teacher's challenge I had a painful awareness that someone much bigger than the teacher was saying the same to me, 'Badly done Hilary, badly done.' There was somebody out there. Even though they were vague and unfathomable, it was almost as though God had been lying on the ground hurting and I had walked past and kicked him. He was not pleased with me and it hurt.

The sharp pain of judgement left me feeling deeply ashamed. The teacher we'd destroyed left and had his nervous break-down and never went back into teaching. I didn't give God another thought until the next time he revealed himself to me in what I have always remembered as the most real encounter of them all. This time it was just me and God. He was not speaking through anyone else; he was, for the first time in my life, speaking directly to me. It was a beautiful summer evening and I was about fifteen years old. I had spent the day at an athletics championship and had just been dropped off at school by the bus. Athletics was one of the great loves in my life, along with field hockey and tennis. When I ran I sensed a tremendous freedom and power. It was probably the one area in my life where I felt, 'I can do this.' Like anyone, as part of a team, I could always fluff a hit in hockey or a shot in tennis but when I was running I had a feeling of mastery. When I ran, I ran alone and I knew I could run like the wind. My mother had watched me at a Sports Day at the age of eight and had proudly said that to the lady next to her and I had always believed it.

This particular championship had, in a sense, been the pinnacle of my athletics career. I had won the 100 metres, the

200 metres and the long jump and been awarded with the cup for the best schoolgirl athlete in the district. It was only a small county, but it was my world and as I walked home alone, across the school field, I was soaring. The sun was going down, the shadows were lengthening and I began to look down at my legs and smile to myself. I was triumphant, but I was overwhelmed with a sense of deep humility. I so vividly remember saying to myself, 'I can run, but it is no thanks to anything I have done, I was given these legs.' And then I heard it, such a gentle whisper, 'I know, I made them and then I gave them to you.' I was overwhelmed with a sense of joy that made me want to burst and shout and run. I did none of those things. I simply floated home as if in a bubble, blown by a gentle breeze that beautiful evening in July. 'Did you win?' my mum called as I opened the front door. 'Yes,' I replied as I headed to my room with a secret I would keep hidden for many years to come. Even now, nearly thirty years later I still hold this as one of my most exhilarating and searing encounters with God.

As I left school and went off to university I found I was free to explore ideas and concepts I had previously blanked off by categorising people and their beliefs in neat, nothing-to-do-with-my-life, little boxes. There I met a young man who talked to me about God as someone he knew personally. I was amazed. God had always been out there somewhere. He had thrilled me, shamed me, shouted at me and whispered to me, but he came and went and surely he could not be captured within the confines of a relationship with another human being. Here was someone who loved God and more amazingly to me was utterly confident of God's love for him.

I hungered for real love. My parents had split up after twenty-five years of marriage and although I so wanted to believe in a love that would last for ever, I had resigned myself to the fact that it was probably not humanly possible. I had swung between Shakespeare's love being 'an ever fixed mark that looks on tempests and is never shaken' and his cynical, 'What is love 'tis not here after, present mirth hath present laughter.' I had wallowed in the popular song, *Plaisir d'amour* which maintained, 'Plaisir d'amour ne dura qu'un moment, Chagrin d'amour dura toute la vie.' (The joys of love only last a moment; the pain of love lasts a whole life through.) Relationships that ended in hurt, had become part of life's pattern and I was scared to even consider that things could be different.

During my last holiday at home, when my parents were still together, I had my last two glimpses of God before I made the decision to pursue him and see if I could catch up with him, rather than being sprung on completely out of the blue (literally at times!). I was watching a programme on the television one day, when I suddenly heard people talking about knowing God. One of them was an actor and one was a policeman. I didn't know 'real' people like this could know God. Ministers were supposed to know God, but I had always considered them to be fakes and completely unapproachable. These people were young and intelligent with a light in their eyes which celebrated life. They bubbled with enthusiasm and confidence before an interviewer who was left looking decidedly nonplussed.

I left the television and the house and went for a walk. My parents have given me a love for the countryside and to this day there is nowhere I would rather be. It had been snowing and for the first time in my life I really *saw* the snow. I saw its whiteness, its tiny glittering crystals. I felt its cold. I saw the vast white blanket spread across the fields and hills so effortlessly and perfectly. I looked at the tree I was standing beside and it was as though someone had taken the time to scatter snow on each twig, outlining it and making it feel important in the vast whiteness. I finally verbalised my longing. 'If only someone had made all this. If only there was a source of life. Could it be possible?' The thought of there being a maker, who had always been there, who had made everything I had ever seen, was at once exhilarating and incredibly peaceful and for the first time in my life, although fleeting, I had a sense of belonging.

Church had put me off God. The work of his hands was what had finally begun to draw me to find the source, the spring from which all life, including mine, had come. I somehow sense that the woman who approached the well, in the heat of the day, had also become disillusioned with religion as she had known it. The belief system in which she had grown up had not satisfied her, it had simply confused her and left her with a sense of longing which it would seem she had tried to dispel through human relationships. I do not know if she had ever sensed that she had glimpsed God. The religious leaders, who represented God in her society, had probably made her feel she was not good enough for him because by her behaviour she had disqualified herself and moved beyond his reach. How wrong they would have been. God does not just reveal himself to people sitting in pews in churches. (And don't worry I do now actually believe he can be found in Anglican churches!) He reveals himself to the hungry and thirsty wherever they may be. It has been said that this woman came to the well and was introduced to the spring. Unwittingly she had gathered together the clues, now it was time to find the treasure. Never let anyone belittle what you would call your glimpses of God, but have the courage to piece them together until they all merge into one wonderful image and you realise, to your absolute amazement, that as Jesus said to the woman, 'I who speak to you am he.' (I have whispered to you all these years, and patiently waited to meet you, and here we are at last: face to face!)

Chapter 3

Who Do You Think You Are?

'You are a Jew and I am a Samaritan woman . . .'

Everyone you meet has a history or a herstory! You only see the outside of the body, on a certain day, standing before you, but it has taken years for that person to become what you see. Some people are confident and outward-looking; some are defeated and introspective. It is all too easy to think that their behaviour and attitude is a response to you at that given moment, when it is in fact the result of all that they have experienced up to the point of meeting you. You can come away from an encounter thinking, 'She was a bit abrupt, I wonder if I was unfriendly or said something to offend?' You have done nothing but you have seen a tiny part of the many complexities of that individual's personality that were formed long before they ever met you. Few of us are wise enough, discerning enough or unselfish enough to see people as they really are, without allowing our own needs and insecurities to get in the way. Jesus sees people as they really are. Whatever a person presents to him, he sees behind and beneath and beyond, with a piercing clarity which eventually leads them to realise he knows them better than they know themselves.

Not only do others not know who we are; we do not know ourselves. The woman at the well is typical of all of us. She is the product of a certain society in a certain place and in a certain time in history. Like us, she has absorbed many of its beliefs and prejudices. The way she sees herself has been determined by those around her and likewise the way she sees other people is a result of conditioning. She is not free to assess each person she meets, with a completely free mind; she pigeon holes and labels them, as we all do. Her beliefs about herself have been drip fed into her from an early age. She has absorbed them and now owns them probably without ever having stood back to objectively assess what she, personally, really thinks.

We are all a product of the world we have been brought up in, where, for most people, our family and our school have had the greatest influence on not just who we are but who we think we are. You may be extremely gifted in any given area, but if your parents told you 'You are hopeless, you'll never make anything of yourself', then in all probability you will not have made anything of yourself. Your gifts are still there; you are potentially very musical, sporty, intelligent or mechanical for example. That's who you are, but who you *think* you are is who you have actually become – unsure, lacking in confidence, critical, negative and unable to encourage anyone else. On the other hand you may not have what the world would recognise as natural talents, but you have been loved, affirmed, encouraged and accepted from the moment you were born and so you have grown up to be friendly, encouraging and able to release talents in others that you do not possess.

Most of us have vivid memories of school. We remember the teachers who brought the best out of us and those who flattened us. I have always loved sport, but I had a wonderful Physical Education teacher who made me believe I could take on anyone and win (with plenty of hard work and training). I also loved the idea of drawing and painting, until I was so humiliated by an art teacher at the age of about thirteen that I have never had the confidence to wield a paintbrush again! I may not have been the best artist, but encouragement would have brought the best out of me. I know many people who have grown up believing they can't do this or that simply because of one comment from one person on one particular day years ago. I saw a wonderful television programme recently on people who had reached the age of one hundred. They were all incredibly active: dancing, fixing motorbikes, playing bowls. One lady was painting the most beautiful watercolour pictures. 'I never believed I was any good at art when I was at school,' she said. It had taken about ninety years to shed an opinion someone else had had about her and to discover something that had lain dormant all those years.

The woman who met Jesus at the well was so burdened by the labelling and opinions of the society she lived in, I am surprised she could even drag herself along to make this daily journey. She was, however, unaware how much she had absorbed from the culture she lived in and more importantly she had probably never realised there could be an alternative. I heard a story recently of a little boy whose behaviour was extremely disruptive and uncontrollable. He was constantly being moved from school to school and no teacher made any headway with him at all, that is, until he met the teacher who greeted him with these words as he walked into her classroom: 'I have heard all about your reputation . . .' There was a pause has he braced himself for the inevitable, but it didn't come. Instead he heard these words: ' And I don't believe a word of it.' He was being given a new start for the first time in his life, and he took it.

When Jesus met this woman, in the heat of the noonday sun in the middle of Samaria, he gave her the chance of a new start and she took it, but first she had to see who she really was in the midst of all the beliefs that had defined her identity as a woman and as a Samaritan. Until she could identify what had locked her into certain thought patterns and attitudes, she would never be free to think for herself and therefore to make her own choices. We are all victims of something or other that has not been our choice; our choice is whether or not we remain victims when we are offered an alternative.

What was the problem with being a Samaritan woman? Many of John's seemingly throwaway comments, in his Gospel, are loaded with a history of conflict that had gone on between Jews and Samaritans for years and also with the tension between the role and status of men and women. Let us look at the Samaritan issue first. John seems to find it necessary to explain what Jesus is doing in this particular area and so he says: '. . . he left Judea and went back once more to Galilee. Now he had to go through Samaria' (Jn. 4:3b–4). At first glance this does not seem unusual. If you look at a map, Judea is in the South, Galilee is in the North and to get from one to the other it is necessary to go through Samaria. However, this was certainly not the route that most Jews would take for as John simply says: '(. . . Jews do not associate with Samaritans)' (Jn. 4:9b).

Jews wholeheartedly despised Samaritans. Jesus knew that and the woman knew that. But although Jesus was a Jew, he has not influenced by the prejudice of the society that surrounded him. He had to go through Samaria because he had to meet this woman. If he had skirted round the district, as most Jews did, then she would have been deprived of the opportunity of her one-on-one encounter with God. He took each person at face value aware of their race and heritage but never judging them for it, or using it as a weapon against them. Jesus saw beyond, to the real person, while being acutely aware that that person is a product of their race. Racial prejudice is ingrained in society. Efforts to legislate against it may help, but they do not eradicate it. We judge, we stereotype people, we subconsciously absorb negative attitudes and we find ourselves easily threatened by someone who is different from us.

When Jesus not only talks to the Samaritan woman, but also asks her for a drink, she is completely thrown. ' "You are a Jew and I am a Samaritan woman. How can you ask me for a drink?" ' (Jn. 4:9a). She knew the conflict between the two races had been going on for years. She may well not have known where and how it started, as with many others who are caught up in nationalistic stalemates. In around 722/721 BC, the king of Assyria transported a group of people to Northern Israel to replace the exiled natural population after the fall of Samaria. Not all the Jews had been exiled and those remaining intermarried with the settlers. The Samaritan race was a result of these mixed marriages and therefore their very existence was a violation of God's law, which commanded his people to remain separate from the people in the lands they inhabited. A baby conceived in the back of a taxi after a drunken night at a party is also a violation of God's law, but God still loves that person and has purposes for them as an individual. His laws were set up for our good and for our protection. We are told to love him, because when we love God we find our place and fulfilment in the universe. When we break those laws, we always damage ourselves, others and our relationship with him. We never sin in isolation. Those couples who intermarried all those hundreds of years before, because it felt good even though it was wrong, had no idea that their actions would have repercussions all down the years. They had no idea that this woman would have problems relating to Jews all her life, leaving her feeling ostracised and inadequate in her own land. Our actions are like the pebble that falls in the pond: the ripples spread far and wide and once the momentum has started it is impossible to stop. That is unless you met Jesus sitting by the well!

Jesus' willingness to walk through, linger in and talk to the inhabitants of this region was a very loud statement against the prejudice ingrained by history. Although he had told his disciples to stay away from Samaria (Mt. 10:5–7), his approach to Samaritans is utterly consistent. Maybe, until the time was right for them to be confronted, he protected his disciples and did not push them into situations that their own prejudice would render them incapable of dealing with. Jesus visits a Samaritan village (Lk. 9:52), he talks to this woman on her home turf and he tells the story of the Good Samaritan (Lk. 10), showing him in an extremely favourable light. When he heals the ten lepers (Lk. 10) it is pointed out that it is only the Samaritan who says thank you, and finally, when we get into the book of Acts, it is as though he feels it is time for the disciples to grow up and he actually sends them to Samaria (though this time, when they go, it will be in the power of the Holy Spirit).

Apart from conflict over the original racial integration and disobedience to God that it displayed, there was also a great deal of conflict over the different practices that the Samaritans followed. Some of them had been influenced by the Jews who had remained in Samaria and they worshipped Jehovah, but they did not do it in the same place or with reference to the same scriptures. Samaritans only believed in and used the Pentateuch (the first five books of the Old Testament), they rejected the writings of the prophets, the psalms, the historical books, etc. The Jews saw this as inadequate. They used the whole of the Old Testament to understand the character of the God they worshipped. It was this limited use of Scripture to which Jesus was probably referring when he said to the woman, 'You Samaritans worship what you do not know' (Jn. 4:22a).

It was not only the basis of their worship which put them at odds with the Jews, but also their place of worship. In around 400 BC the Samaritans had built a temple on Mount Gerazim, which of course the Jews had never acknowledged as a legitimate place to worship God. As far as they were concerned there could only be one place for a temple.

> Destroy completely all the places on the high mountains and on the hills and under every spreading tree where the nations you are dispossessing worship their gods. . . . You must not worship the Lord your God in their way. But you are to seek the place the Lord your God will choose from among all the tribes to put his name there for his dwelling. To that place you must go . . . (Deut. 12:2, 4–5).

The woman expected Jesus to tow the Jewish party line on this issue, 'Our fathers worshipped on this mountain, but you Jews claim that the place where we must worship is in Jerusalem' (Jn. 4:21). As we will see later, Jesus' idea of worship was far greater than going to a certain place, at a certain time, to say certain things. He would speak of freedom and the spirit, a concept she had never entertained because of the expectations and limitations placed on her by the only religion she had known. How many people give up on God because they hate the religion of their family or their country? It is so easy to throw the 'baby out with the bath water'; to reject what the society you have been brought up in has embraced as normal and not be open to considering anything else. This stance may give the illusion that you are free, however, by reacting, rather than responding in a considered way, you place huge limitations on yourself and make it hard to ever see or hear God who is far bigger and personal than any religious system.

Not only do some reject God because of the religion they are brought up with, but some also make the mistake of thinking they are all right with God because of their society's or family's tradition. Jews and Samaritans both claimed a direct line back to Jacob, only through a different route! Here was a Jew sitting on Jacob's well and a Samaritan coming to drop her bucket in it. She felt she had a right to be there, through Ephraim and Manasseh she had a direct link to the father of the chosen race and therefore to God. No one has a direct link to God. It doesn't matter what family or country we are born into, we each stand before God as individuals and we each choose to accept or reject him as our loving father. It has been said, 'Being born in a garage doesn't make you a car.' Being born in a so-called Christian country does not make you a Christian. There has to be that moment when we hear Jesus himself say, 'I who speak to you am he', and we need to say, 'I who listen to you am me!' not a white person or a British person or someone who has been brought up a Catholic, but simply me!

To be a woman in a Jewish environment was hard. To be a Samaritan in a Jewish environment was uncomfortable, but to be a Samaritan woman was considered the pits on those two counts: race and gender. To be a divorced Samaritan woman did not bear thinking about! Let's look first at what it meant simply to be a woman in that day and age. Jewish women grew up believing they were inferior to men. They obeyed their fathers without question and then moved into marriage to obey their husbands. In Genesis, Eve had been told, 'Your desire will be for your husband and he will rule over you' (Gen. 3:16), and this is exactly what happened. There has been much debate about whether this was a decree about what *should* happen, or an observation of what *would* happen, as a result of the Fall. The Samaritan woman would never have taken part in the debate, or even heard of it! She would have no concept of woman's rights in the face of male chauvinism. Women had very few rights; their legal position was much weaker than that of the men.

A man could divorce his wife if he 'found some uncleanness in her' or apparently if she burnt the toast, but on no account could a woman divorce her husband. Maybe this poor lady (with five divorces) had a faulty toaster! A woman suspected of unfaithfulness had to take a jealousy test; there was no such test for a man. 'This was a "trial by ordeal" typical of ancient Near Eastern culture. The woman was made to drink bitter water. If she were innocent, then the water did not affect her. If she were guilty, she would become ill. In that case she was stoned to death as an adulteress.' (Shame if you happened to have a stomach upset the day of the trial!) A woman could be sold by her father to pay off a debt and unlike a man, she could not be freed after six years. Although women, and particularly widows, were afforded some protection within Jewish society, on the whole their rights were usually overlooked or deliberately curtailed. It is not surprising in a culture where the men actually prayed, 'Blessed art thou, O Lord . . . who hast not made me a woman,' that by New Testament times women had stopped being active in temple or synagogue worship. They had never taken any leadership role or been allowed into the holy of holies, so perhaps they had simply got fed up. (Modern churches that leave their women on the fringes without a voice should take note.)[1] The very fact that this woman shows an interest in worship, against all the odds, shows tenacity and courage as far as I can see. It is no wonder, however, that she is extremely wary when this tired Jewish man even makes eye contact, never mind making a request for a drink from her. Not only would a rabbi not talk to a woman he did not know in the street, he would not even talk to his own wife if he met her in the street! This was certainly no ordinary rabbi, and he showed it, not by standing up and denouncing a system he so obviously deplored, but by simply loving, by building a bridge to an isolated woman and allowing her to walk across it to meet him half way.

So what did it mean not just being a woman in that society, but being a Samaritan woman? To Jewish men Samaritan women were the lowest of the low. They were brought up believing that 'The daughters of the Samaritans are [deemed as unclean] menstruants from their cradle' (Mishna, *Nidd.* 4:1).[2] What a horrendously insulting and humiliating image! With that in mind they would proudly look down on Samaritan women and, judging them ceremonially unclean, would have nothing to do with them. What an understatement when John writes that on the disciples' return from going to find food, they 'were surprised to see him talking with a woman'. Surprised! They must have been flabbergasted, but they had the wit to keep their mouths shut. 'No one asked, "What do you want?" or "Why are you talking with her?" ' This man they had chosen to follow was certainly going to turn their world of prejudice upside-down.

They had not been there to hear Jesus' simple request to the woman, 'Will you give me a drink?' It seemed so innocent, however those few words blew hundreds of years of prejudice out of the water! He was associating with this woman, who the rest of the male Jewish population saw only as scum, and more than that he was asking for a drink. She would draw the water in her bucket and pass it to him with her hands. The Jews had legislated against this very sharing of utensils to avoid contamination. They maintained that 'a Samaritan conveys uncleanness by what he lies, sits or rides on, by his spittle (including the phlegm of his lungs, throat, or nose) and by his urine. . . .'[3]

If you look carefully at the incident you will realise the double standard adopted by the disciples. They would never share utensils with Samaritans, yet they had just gone into town to buy food and unless they walked a very long way, they must have bought it from Samaritans, presumably hoping they hadn't spat on it! How like us they are. We can sit in judgement on regimes and practices and say we would have nothing to do with them, yet when it suits our needs and our desire of the moment we find it so easy to abandon our scruples. How many of us buy the latest designer running shoes, knowing full well that we are paying over $100 for something someone, maybe even a child, has been paid $4 to make in some ghastly sweatshop in the Far East. When it comes down to it we care more about our image, which must sport the right logo, than we do about the child who is the victim of an evil and very well-established commercial racket.

So these disciples returned with their 'Samaritan' food to find Jesus talking to a woman, a Samaritan woman and unknown to them at this point, a divorced Samaritan woman. Here was the third stigma which she carried for all to see. As I have already said, a woman had no right to divorce her husband. Her only way out of any unbearable situation was to approach the court to get him to divorce her, probably at the cost of her dignity and integrity as she would no doubt have to admit to things she had not done. Sometimes women actually paid their husbands or did things that would induce them to agree to a divorce. In theory a woman was allowed to remarry as many times as she liked after a legal divorce, but in practice two or at most three remarriages were considered the absolute maximum. No wonder this woman came to the well when there was no one else around. Local men and women would no doubt have looked down on her, and her five failed marriages, with utter contempt; Jesus did not.

No matter who you are, no matter where you are coming from, no matter how much baggage you carry from the society you have been brought up in, it is possible to put down the water pot of other peoples' condemnation and expectations about your role in life and make a new start. If you had asked that woman, 'Who do you think you are?', she would probably have come up with a list: a woman, a Samaritan woman, a divorced Samaritan woman, an unmarried, divorced Samaritan woman, and if she had been really honest she would have added all the hurt that went with each of those 'titles', an unclean, unworthy, unloved, unimportant, unmarried, divorced Samaritan woman.

How long is your list? What would you honestly answer to that question, 'Who do you think you are?' We will never fully appreciate the way Jesus really sees us in the present until we are willing to be honest about who we really are, as a result of where we have come from, in other words, what has happened in our past. This woman had dragged the burden of other peoples' opinions around with her basically from birth, but she was not simply a victim and Jesus shows that in order to walk away from her past she has to be willing to be honest about her present and to accept personal responsibility for those areas of her life that she is so keen to hide. She has a skeleton in the cupboard. I am sure the man she lived with would not like to be referred to as such, but he needed bringing out into the open!

Chapter 4

Prisoner of the Past

'I have no husband. . . .'

Someone asked me one day, 'What has the greatest influence on who you are today: the way you see your past or the way you see your future?' They were really saying, are you happy now because of the hand that life has dealt you up to this point or because you are so sure of the positive future which awaits you? Are you sad because of what lies behind you or because of your fears for the future, your feeling that maybe you have no future? Our state of mind is deeply affected by more than the weather! We are all suspended between where we have been and where we are going; it is called the present. No moment in time stands alone; it is determined by what has preceded and what will follow it. Today I may be very happy because yesterday I was successful at a job interview. Today I may be fearful because tomorrow I will hear the result of a brain scan. If we are ever to understand ourselves and those we come into contact with we need to be aware of the effect on all of us of being suspended between these two worlds.

Jesus' conversation with the woman at the well reveals his awareness of how her past and the vague ideas she had about the future were affecting her. In this chapter we will concentrate on the past and in later chapters, on the present and the future. We have already seen that to all intents and purposes she was a prisoner of the past. She was locked in by the opinions of others, attitudes towards her which ironically ensured that she kept her reputation even if she had ever wanted to shed it. She went to the well when there was no one else around (Jn. 4:6). She could not escape the prison, but she could avoid people passing her cell and throwing insults through the bars.

She was locked in by the deep-rooted tradition of institution-alised racism (Jn. 4:9). As we have seen, Jews did not mix with Samaritans. Most of the time she probably protected herself from the implications of this prejudice by staying within Samaria. This was a stalemate which had been in place for years. It takes tremendous courage and energy to challenge the status quo of hatred and the majority of us do not have enough of either, so we simply put up with a system even though it appals us. Those in Northern Ireland, who are trying to over-throw years of inbred bigotry, not dissimilar to that so firmly established between Jews and Samaritans, can only be admired.

The woman was locked into a limited belief system. She is confused by what she has been told, but it has to suffice because she thinks she has no way of knowing what is actually true. 'Our fathers worshipped on this mountain, but you Jews claim that the place where we must worship is in Jerusalem' (Jn. 4:19). She is not unaware of the beliefs of others, but she is not free to consider them objectively because she has been so influenced by the beliefs of her own culture. These don't satisfy her, they simply fill the religious slot in her mind and lull her into thinking that she has no need to seriously consider any alternative. I think it was Billy Graham who said, 'Most of us have been inoculated with just enough religion to prevent us ever catching the real thing!'

The most subtle prison, in which the woman at the well found herself, was her cycle of behaviour. Whether she wanted to or not she seemed unable to free herself from the cycle of broken relationships. How many of us have behaviour patterns, which we hate and even despise, but which, in our own strength, we cannot walk away from? We do what we do in the present because of what has happened to us in our past and we reach the awful conclusion that there is no escape. Although she had never voiced it, I am sure this woman longed for an new start. So did I. When I became a Christian I thought that was what I was getting, but I very soon discovered it was not that simple.

I became a Christian at the age of nineteen. It was the end of the long journey I referred to in Chapter 2. My parents had separated and in my loneliness I simply sat in the garden one day in July 1975 and admitted to God that I really did believe in him and if he wasn't tired of all my dithering then I would desperately like him to move into my life. I didn't fully understand the implications of what that meant and I am still learning, but I knew there was nothing I wanted more than his closeness. I didn't want a crutch to prop me up after the painful collapse of my parents' marriage; I wanted much more than that. I wanted a life, a new life, a new start, not just a crutch that would enable me to carry on hobbling along.

I didn't hear a voice, I didn't feel any wind, other than the gentle summer breeze blowing in the garden, but I knew I belonged. For a long time I had been a long way from home and that afternoon I had found my way back to my maker. At first I was thrilled with the knowledge that I was forgiven and with the wonderful privilege of being able to speak to God, not only about all the things in my life that I could not share with anyone else, but also about all the people I loved and cared for. I was excited to be able to intercede for others, but my excitement with this new found intercessory role led to a presumption about people's lives and a boldness in their lives which was not always appreciated. From being an intercessor, I soon became an intermediary, and then the solution to people's problems. On that sunny summer's afternoon I realised that I had been misguided in thinking I was the solution to the problems in my family; God wanted me to bring my burdens to him. After a long talk to an uncle one day, we had reached a stalemate. God was now very real to me and I wanted him to be real to my uncle. He was very obviously getting fed up with our conversation so reluctantly I brought it to a close by saying, 'I will pray for you.' 'You needn't bother,' he quickly retorted. Twenty-five years have now passed and we have never spoken together about God since. I had been too keen to tell him where I was before listening to where he was coming from.

It all seemed so black and white at the beginning. I took God at his word. If I confessed then I would be forgiven. If I stood up for God I would be knocked down. If I needed help he would be my refuge. I finished my English Literature degree, did my postgraduate certificate in education, squeezed in a year teaching English at a high school in Nottingham and then got married. That first year of marriage was one of the hardest years of my life. Not because of my husband, but because of me – I was a mess.

We spent that first year travelling, with two extended stays in Canada and Australia. People were so envious as they waved us off on what everyone called a year-long honeymoon. I was not naive. I had listened to Dr Redpath, a wonderful teacher and preacher, when he spoke to us on our wedding saying, 'This first year will not be easy, you will have your struggles, but do not let the sun go down on your anger.' How wise he was. I soon realised the sun needed to stay permanently in the sky! I was full of anger and had not been aware of the hold it had on my life.

When we arrived in Canada, my luggage had been lost en route, so I had no clothes, but I had enough mental and emotional baggage to keep me going for months. Its contents just kept spilling out, more often than not all over Charles, and I had to face the awful truth that although we had travelled hundreds of miles across the Atlantic and were now sitting on an idyllic island in the gulf stream off the west coast of Canada, things were far from idyllic. I had brought my past with me. I could have travelled to the moon and back and it would still raise its ugly head and dictate my pretty horrible behaviour. I could not escape me.

Words from the Bible, which had seemed so obvious at first and so true, were not true for me. One day I read, 'If the son sets you free, you will be free indeed' (Jn. 8:36). When I first became a Christian I had known that freedom, what was wrong with me now? I had been given a new start; I was married and I had a new place to live in Canada and I was miserable. I was constantly spoiling for a fight and causing arguments with my husband. He had only ever seen his parents disagree once (and even then his dad had later apologised in front of all the children) and I don't think he knew what had hit him. The behaviour patterns I had hated in England were there in full force in Canada. I was so like the chickens I heard about in the very apt little story that follows.

One day a Hindu priest was browsing round a market in a village in India when he came to a stall selling chickens. Each chicken was tied to a central pole by a piece of string looped round its neck. The chickens walked round and round the pole one behind the other with no prospect of any escape except into the cooking pot. The priest was horrified at the undignified way these precious creatures were being treated and so, on a moment's impulse, he bought them all. He lead them, by their pieces of string, to the nearest large field outside the village and with a big smile removed the loop from each neck and let them go. How thrilled he must have been to see his mission accomplished as they took off into the air and flew, no doubt with smiles on their faces too. How sad he must have been as he watched them all come down out of the sky after about two hundred metres of freedom, only to alight in the field and start walking round in a circle again. (No longer with smiles on their faces!)

How many of us are given the chance of a new start and find we are unable to take it? We are prisoners of the past. We may want to behave differently and we may be given every opportunity to start again, but it just doesn't happen. All of us face this problem. I faced it on an island in Canada, the apostle Paul (no less!) faced it as he wrote his letter to the Romans:

I do not understand what I do. For what I want to do I do not do, but what I hate I do. . . . For I have the desire to do what is good, but I cannot carry it out. For what I do is not the good I want to do . . . (Rom. 7:15, 18–19a).

Paul goes on to discover the solution; why is it that so many of us never do? We hate the way we are, we deplore our attitudes and behaviour, which is usually at its worst with those we love the most, and we fail to identify the root of our problems. Those poor little boys who have been unfortunate enough to watch their fathers beating their mothers are more likely to become wife beaters than those who have never witnessed such an awful happening. Surely they don't go into marriage intent on beating their wives? Let me give you another illustration from my own experience.

For many years of my life, and especially since I have had children, I have struggled with Christmas. In theory I love the celebration and the presents, but as the day approaches I find myself becoming uptight and unreasonable. I am not relaxed and consequently those around me end up being put under great pressure. Why am I like this? Is it because I don't like the commercialism of Christmas? No. It is because I have such mixed memories of this special day from my childhood. No one was unkind at Christmas, on the contrary, they made everything special and happy. I have wonderful memories of being told, 'You can't come in', from behind the closed door where I could hear my mum wrapping presents. But, I can vividly recall going up to bed at the end of Christmas day, as late as I could make it, knowing that in the morning it would all be different; the magic would have gone and tension would have re-established itself. I wanted Father Christmas and all the joy and love associated with him to stay all year and when he didn't I channelled my sense of disappointment towards my parents. Now as I look back I realise I was longing for the heart of Christmas, the Christ child in the manger, who was from all eternity and who will be for ever, but at that time I did not know him and my sense of loss when it was all over was palpable. Now I have my own children, I want to make Christmas the most wonderful day, celebrating the beauty of the gift of Jesus through our own giving, but my desire is so strong that if I am not careful, my expectations become too high and I destroy the very thing I am trying to do.

One day I heard a speaker, called Jerry Root, explaining my dilemma and I discovered there is actually a name for it! He said that many of us have lives like scratched records. There was a point that we were hurt and the scratch was made. In the years to come we will continually get stuck at that point. When a record gets stuck it plays the same few bars of music or words over and over again. (Use your imagination and go back in time to LPs, before the wonders of modern technology!) The needle gets stuck in the groove and cannot move on unless someone lifts it out and puts it down further on. I was repeating the moment where I felt the scratch of intense disappointment, hoping that somehow I would move on. This kind of behaviour is called 'Repetition in search of mastery' and I have tried it in so many areas of my life. You set up the same situation over and over again believing that this time you will be victorious.

I believe the woman who met Jesus at the well would have known exactly what I was talking about. Why on earth do people stagger from one failed relationship to another? Not because they think they are going to fail again, but because they hope to succeed. I hate doing what I do but I launch myself into the all too familiar scenario, believing I can conquer it. For some people the fight to win and move on is too difficult and they have to conclude there is no escape. It is at this point that they resort to anaesthetising behaviour such as drink and drugs, simply to protect themselves from hurt that has become unbearable. Thank God I have never gone down that road, but I have certainly known and sometimes still know the despair of fighting the losing battle against self. As I sat on that island in Canada, I knew there was nowhere to run to, literally, and there was nowhere to hide; I had to find some solutions to this problem of the past for Charles' sake as well as my own: One day I heard someone quoting this verse on the radio and I thought, here is my answer, 'Forgetting what is behind and straining towards what is ahead I press on toward the goal' (Phil. 3:13). I had lost my goal and if I could only get it back again then things would be all right. I had given up a very good teaching job to get married. I had been part of a vibrant, go-ahead English department in a large comprehensive and I had to acknowledge that I was resentful about being expected to cut my career so short. I know it was my choice, but I had made it knowing I still had the goal of marriage. Now I was married and suddenly I had, probably for the first time in my life, no goals. At this point I was not mature enough to say with Paul, '. . . we make it our goal to please him' (2 Cor. 5:9). With no obvious future to look forward to, I found myself drawn continually to my past. I spent many hours on my own while Charles was lecturing or studying and I found my own company very uncomfortable. 'When you are on your own your mind will always gravitate towards unresolved pain' (J. Root). Why was my past giving me such a hard time?

I believe there are two mistakes most of us make when we look back at the past. Either we idealise it and convince ourselves that it was so good then that we *won't* let go (we may be given the challenge to move on and change, but we won't), or we remember it as being so bad that, much as we would love to, we *can't* let go (we dream of change, but we can't make it happen). Both attitudes prevent us from living with a sense of freedom in the present and restrict any chance of moving into a new future.

Let us explore these attitudes for a moment. The first one comes under the heading:

Remember the good old days

Have you ever heard yourself saying that? I used to think it was only older people who were guilty of comparing the present with the past and always concluding that the past was so much better. However, I was very young when I heard myself saying, 'Remember the good old days' for the first time. On returning from our 'year-long honeymoon' I went back to teach at the school in which I had been a pupil. It was a bizarre experience for many reasons, least of all the experience of finding my memory was playing tricks! I now sat on this side of the teacher's desk instead of that side and as I watched the fifteen-year-old girls filing into my classroom I found myself thinking, 'My goodness, look at the length of those skirts! They were never so short in my day. What has happened to standards and any sense of modesty?' It wasn't long after I had wallowed in this self-righteous attitude that I happened to come upon my old school skirt in a bag in the attic. I couldn't resist and I held it up to see if it would still fit! Help! I never remembered it being that short! Now I came to think about it though, I do remember my mum saying to me, 'Don't you think it is a little embarrassing for the male teachers to have to walk up the stairs behind you in a skirt like that?' and I do remember just smiling and thinking, 'How stuffy the older generation are.'

I was amazed to discover in the Bible that people have obviously been prattling on about the good old days for a very long time and God has never been impressed. 'Do not say, "Why were the good old days better than these," ' he warns in Ecclesiastes 7:9, ' ". . . for it is not good to ask such questions." ' The British as a nation are very nostalgic. We are forced to be in some things like soccer, for example, for it is only in the very distant past that we actually won at world level and how we long for those glory days again! I mean, hang it all chaps, we had an Empire all to ourselves once, we were Britannia and we ruled! We still celebrate that lost era every year in a musical event known as The Last Night of the Proms with a hearty rendition of *Land of Hope and Glory*. We build new estates with mock-Tudor and mock-Georgian semi-detached houses, we wallow in the romantic world of *Crabtree and Evelyn* and *Laura Ashley* and, as one journalist recently commented in *The Times*, 'It is time we said, "Stop the world – we want to get on." '[4] He sees the whole nation as having a Peter Pan syndrome, maintaining that 'We cling to our past because it is a comfort-blanket and we don't want to grow up and face the real world.'

Here I plead guilty. Although I dislike mock-Tudor houses and the last night of the Proms, I have always dreamed of living in the olden days, of dressing like a real lady and of never having my quiet, serene world rudely interrupted by phone, fax and e-mail. One day, would you believe it, my dream actually came true! About twelve years ago a spoof Sherlock Holmes film was being filmed in the beautiful Lake District, in the north of England. They needed extras and the chance to 'co-star' with the famous actors, Michael Caine and Ben Kingsley, saw me rushing off to try for a part. My face fitted, for some reason, costumes were measured and we reported for filming at first light the next day. What fun! Now I could wear a long dress, a feathered hat, a shawl and beneath it all corsets, long knickers, a bustle, and dainty boots. I was back in the past and I was there with a real swish in my skirts and a swagger in my walk! That is until we were nearing the end of the second day of shooting (not killing, you understand, I am just showing you how much I got 'into' the film world jargon! Mind you if the producer had been around literal shooting may have been a temptation). I had spent two twelve-hour days on my feet trussed up in the most uncomfortable clothes I had ever worn. Why did he not tell us it was going to hurt so much? My bustle kept slipping. I had a tide mark creeping up my long skirt, because in true Lake District style it had drizzled for nearly the whole time and my ankle boots were shrinking and pinching my poor old modern feet which had spent most of their lives in trainers. I could not wait to get out of all this stuff, slip back into my jeans and back into the present.

'Do not say "Why were the good old days better than these?" For it is not good to ask such questions.' It is not good because it is not true, they weren't! In the days when ladies glided around in long skirts and promenaded through the park with parasols, little boys were being stuffed up chimneys, stuck down coal pits and hidden in half-lit factories so their employers could become richer by the minute and their wives could buy ever more beautiful clothes and finery, which were often laced up so tightly that they permanently damaged their internal organs!

Not only does looking back and romanticising encourage myths about the past, it also leads to a real sense of ingratitude for the present. Instead of enjoying what we have now and being thankful for where we are now, we compare them, and the present usually comes out unfavourably. (And that of course is where the world of advertising steps in, but that is another story- see next chapter!)

Constantly hankering for what was can paralyse us in the present. A vivid illustration of this can be found in the story of Lot's wife in the book of Genesis. Lot, Abraham's nephew, had made some very bad choices in life, which had affected his whole family. Due to his greed and selfishness he had taken them to live in the notorious town of Sodom where they were continually under pressure to become a part of the sinful society all around them. Thanks to the prayers of his faithful uncle, God gave the family the chance to move out, to move on and to make a new start. Unfortunately, on the day they were leaving Mrs Lot did the one thing she had been told not to do; as they made their way from the city now deluged in burning sulphur, she looked back and was immediately turned into a pillar of salt. (You can read the whole story in Genesis 19.) Maybe she had just put out lots of bedding plants and it was so hard to leave that lovely garden she had cultivated for all those years? Just one look back; it wouldn't hurt. When God tells you to move on, don't look back, however unsure you are about what lies ahead, clinging to the security of the past instead of finding security in God will always paralyse you in the present.

We have thought about those who move on reluctantly and *won't* let go, what about those who long to move on but *can't* let go? Hundreds of books have been written on this very subject and therefore anything I say will only scratch the surface, but it might at least enable you to identify how it is that you have got stuck. You may have been given a new start, but unlike the woman who met Jesus at the well, you have been unable to take it. You may well have tried, but have given up and now believe that you will always be a prisoner of the past. There is a well-known story about an elephant which illustrates the point. (I am not sure who to attribute this to as I have heard it from several different people.)

A young elephant was brought in from the jungle and tied to a huge tree stump by an iron chain, which was fastened around his ankle. Wild with anger at the abrupt curtailment of his freedom, the elephant bellowed and pulled at the chain day and night. His tough hide was torn and split as it chaffed on the chain and in time just as the skin was broken, so also was his will. He eventually realised there was no escape and so he gave up trying to bring one about. It was not long before his keepers were able to replace the thick chain with what in comparison was like a thread of cotton. If he had only pulled, the thin rope would have easily snapped. The problem was, the elephant no longer believed he could walk away, so he never tried. His past experience had defeated his present potential and robbed him of any meaningful future.

Letting go of the bad old days

Let's look at this another way. What if you find that you don't want to cling to the past, but the past clings to you. Here are three possible reasons.

Blame

One of the main reasons people cannot leave their past behind is because instead of taking any responsibility for the situation in which they find themselves, they place all the blame on someone else. Of course people have wronged you. Of course people have hurt you. You may have had your innocence snatched from you at a very early age, but if you live the whole of your life feeling you are a victim, you will eventually find you have relinquished all control: you are powerless and if you are honest, you are stuck. You cannot change what has happened to you, but you can change the way you see it and therefore the hold it has on you. I find it fascinating that the thing that caused the woman at the well to hang her head in shame and to avoid people was the very thing that she wanted to tell her fellow townsfolk about after she had talked with Jesus. 'Come, see a man who told me everything I ever did' (Jn. 4:29). Her past had not changed, but with him she had faced it. She did not say, 'Come, see a man who told me everything that ever happened to me' or 'everything I was a victim of,' but 'everything I ever *did*'. Her past had been laid bare and she was acknowledging her part in it all.

Many people live life feeling sorry for themselves and excusing their behaviour with the argument that it is not their fault that they are the way they are. I did it for a while on that island in Canada. It was not my fault I caused arguments and tension in my marriage, I was merely repeating what I believed was the norm. I was tied by a piece of cotton and I did not believe there was any escape. One of my favourite authors is Thomas Hardy. He was miserable, moody and depressive most of his life and that makes him a wonderful writer! The sad thing about Thomas Hardy is that he was also tied by a piece of cotton to an incident that happened in a tiny cottage in Dorset the moment he was born. When baby Thomas appeared, he made no sound and was thought to be dead. He was put aside while the nurse attended to his mother. She then decided to give this baby a chance and dumping him in and out of hot and cold water she managed to produce a cry and that first gasp of breath. Thomas Hardy grew up to be a very unhappy man who was unable to form successful relationships with others. He did not fall in love with his wife until she had died and then it was too late. This made life extremely difficult for his second wife. He excused his depressive behaviour all his life, basically saying, 'It is not my fault I am like this, I was rejected at birth.'

If you find you are chained to your past by huge metal links and have long given up on any thought of escape, then it is time to look at your responsibility, not necessarily for what has happened, although that may well be valid, but more for your *response* to what has happened. Holding on to the right to blame will keep you locked well and truly inside your prison, as will any sense of shame.

To the question who was to blame for the tragedy of a man born blind, Jesus replied that no one was to blame. 'He was born blind so that God's work might be revealed in him' (Jn. 9:3). We spend a lot of energy wondering who can be blamed for our own or other people's tragedies – our parents, ourselves, the immigrants, the Jews, the gays, the blacks, the fundamentalists, the Catholics? There is a strange satisfaction in being able to point our finger at someone, even ourselves. It gives some sort of explanation and it offers us some form of clarity. But Jesus doesn't allow us to solve our own or other people's problems through blame. The challenge he poses us is to discern, in the midst of our darkness, the light of God. In Jesus' vision everything, even the greatest tragedy, can become an occasion in which God's works can be revealed. How radically new my life would be if I were willing to move beyond blaming to proclaiming the works of God in our midst.'[5]

Shame

Shame or guilt is not something to be afraid of, not something to be buried, not something to be dismissed as an underhand way of controlling our children or our society, it is something to be thankful for, because it is God's small voice within us telling us that something is not right. We ignore it at our peril. Like pain, it alerts our whole being to a problem and like pain, it can be deadened and silenced, but not for ever. Whatever has caused a feeling of shame does not go away simply because it is ignored. Many people make 'deathbed confessions' about things that have happened years ago. They are still buried in their consciences and age and distance from the event has not removed its consequences.

The wonderful thing about meeting Christ is that you realise all he wants to do is forgive you and release you from this prison of guilt. I was watching a debate on television one day and my mind was wandering, because it was as airy fairy as usual, until I saw the humanist on the panel lean towards the Christian and say, 'What I envy most about you Christians is your forgiveness. I have no one to forgive me.' Well of course he did, as much as anyone does, but forgiveness does not come cheap. Jesus bought it through his death on the cross. How humbling, the king of the universe was crucified for me and yet I am not humble enough to say I am sorry and to live in the good of that forgiveness. My husband has made this very wise statement (one of many!): 'The only way sin leaves your body is through your mouth'. We actually have to formulate the words and say them. 'If we confess our sins, he is faithful and just and will forgive us our sins and purify us from all unrighteousness' (1 Jn. 1:9). It is not God who keeps us locked in a prison, it may well be our pride.

Hardness of heart

Hardness of heart also keeps us well and truly stuck in the past. Many of us face the battle of being willing to come to God and repent in order to receive forgiveness, but an even greater battle is fought, and usually lost, over being willing to forgive others. I know families where sisters do not speak to each other because of some small incident or word said so many years ago that they have almost forgotten what it was all about. I recently saw the lovely old mother, in a family like this, die without ever seeing the reconciliation of her children. And true to form, they sat on opposite sides of the church at her funeral. How sad and how stupid you might say, I would never bear a grudge like that! Oh really? What about the person down the street you deliberately avoid and the affection for the people you love which you deliberately withhold because of the way they have treated you recently? The root of all bitterness is an unwillingness to forgive. It may grow from a seemingly small, insignificant incident, but its hold can eventually strangle you. 'Unless you forgive you won't be forgiven' (Mt. 6:15), Jesus told his disciples. 'Impossible!' you shout, 'If you knew what they had done to me.' Yes and what makes you such a righteous judge? If we start to live in the warmth and joy of receiving God's forgiveness for the things we have admitted responsibility for, we will begin to discover that a willingness to forgive others just starts to happen. You will still remember the things that have hurt you, but in time the memory and forgiveness will become simultaneous. God enables us to see others as he sees them as sinful human beings in need of forgiveness, and you will find you can't help but forgive.

The woman who met Jesus at the well would no doubt have faced all the issues we have just looked at because they are all part of the struggle of what it means to be a fallen human being trying to make sense of life on a fallen earth. She was locked into repeating patterns of behaviour, deeply rooted in her past, and she realised the way out was not to struggle and try and make a future, but to simply give Jesus room in her present. I said earlier that we are all suspended between the past and the future. For some, that place called the present can be extremely uncomfortable, something to be endured with a grim acceptance or something to be rushed through as quickly as possible, but Jesus has different ideas, as we shall see in the next chapter.

Chapter 5

Living in the Waiting Room

*'Sir, give me this water so I won't get thirsty and
have to keep coming here . . .'*

When life is boring, monotonous and frustrating, most of us,
like the woman at the well, simply keep our heads down and
plod on. She does not admit she is fed up, in so many words,
but the alacrity with which she reaches for what Jesus offers,
reveals how desperate she is for change. She is so obviously
dissatisfied with who she has been, who she is and what she
does and is only to happy to ditch it all when she hears these
words:

> Everyone who drinks this water will be thirsty again, but whoever
> drinks the water I give him will never thirst. Indeed, the water I
> give will become in him a spring of water welling up to eternal life
> (Jn. 4:13–14).

Maybe for the first time in her life she hears there is an
alternative, there is a way out of this daily grind, and she
reaches for it with both hands, 'Sir, give me this water so that I
won't get thirsty and have to keep coming here to draw water'
(Jn. 4:15). In other words, 'Jesus – give me a break!' At this
point she is taking the offer literally. She is drawing from a well
and he is offering a spring. She has yet to discover that his
meaning is spiritual and not literal and he is the spring.

I would say that most of my in-depth conversations are with women, as opposed to men, and the more people I listen to, the more aware I have become of how dissatisfied many (if not most) women are. I am not just speaking here of women who do not know Christ, but also of women who do. There are an awful lot of discontented Christian women. I know, they are not only out there, they are also in here, they are at times, me! Being dissatisfied can so easily become a way of life. Listen to yourself on the phone or when you meet friends in the street. Do you encourage them and rejoice in our present circumstances, or do you moan and groan, paint as bleak a picture as you can and then show what a stalwart you are for soldiering on.

So many of us live in our own strength and accept the frustration and failure that brings, with a grim determination which may well impress others, but is not in the slightest bit honouring to God. We draw on our own pathetically inadequate resources, filling our little bucket at the same little well, when there is a whole ocean to draw on. Jesus wants us to come to the spring, more than that, he wants the spring to actually flow from within us. A spring is always fresh, it never stops flowing, a little bucket with a few drops in the bottom runs out so quickly and when there is a hole in the bucket it makes things even worse! How many of us spend our lives patching the holes in our buckets and wondering why we are never satisfied and why we never have anything to offer to the thirsty souls around us?

Is it only contemporary women who struggle with discontentment as they try and buy into the *You can have it all* dream? (There has actually been a book published with this title.) I think not. It isn't only the lure of online shopping that cons us into thinking, 'I've just got to have that!' The desire for more because I have got less has been around since the beginning of time. Look at the first woman – seemingly she had everything (and a bag to put it in as my wonderful old Granny used to say!), but everything just wasn't enough.

If you had been a fly on the wall in the garden of Eden (which you wouldn't have been because I am sure there were no flies and probably no walls, but if you had *peeped* in to the garden of Eden . . .), you would have thought, 'This is all anyone could ever long for, what a lucky woman to live there.' Eve lived in a wonderful environment: no pollution, no endangered species, no greenhouse effect, no disease, no death – just perfect. She was healthy, she had plenty to eat (well, plenty of organic vegetables anyway!). She had a fabulous husband with whom she had a oneness never known since. She had been taken from his very being; they were equal and they were one. At this point, there were of course no children and all was bliss. Not that children always wreck the peace and quiet. They can, in fact, be extremely peaceful and calming, they can also, as we all know, create havoc! I remember so well a little incident in our family that illustrates the Jekyll and Hyde ability of most children. Charles had just returned from a trip away and Matthew, aged about four, was enjoying a cuddle with his dad on the settee. As I walked through the lounge, saw the happy scene, and heard Matthew saying, 'I love it when you come home Daddy.' I gloated a little with the thought, 'What a wonderful serene, close loving family we have.' A few moments later I was back in the lounge and how the scene had changed. Matthew was now crouching behind the settee, Charles was hidden (or was it hiding?) behind the newspaper and I heard a little voice mutter, 'I wish you'd go back to where you've come from!' Moving swiftly on, I headed for the kitchen thinking, 'Life would be so much easier without children, or is it without fathers? Oh well, whatever! Time to make the dinner.'

Anyway, Eve did not have any of these problems, she only had Adam and they got on just fine, not only with each other, but also with their heavenly father who obviously walked and talked with them regularly.

Eve was totally satisfied until it was suggested to her that she could *have* more and not only that, she could also *be* more. She had rights and it was time she asserted them. The limits

God had placed on the humans were something to be contested and defied. They were not for their good. Surely he could not be trusted. God was a killjoy. He had not given them everything, he had withheld access to the tree of knowledge of good and evil and if she only gained that, then she would be satisfied. 'But I don't know what you mean by dissatisfied, I have never heard of that word,' she may have feebly whispered to Satan. 'Well, you have now,' he must have chuckled, adding a quiet aside she could not hear, 'and now you'll never be satisfied on this earth again.' Don't be too hard on Eve. She may have been the first, but she is certainly not the last to have said, 'You've given me so much God, I have so much to be grateful for and thanks God, but . . . it is not enough!'

If everything God made was perfect then where did this disquiet come from? How could a bad attitude possibly develop in a place where everything was good? Like a disease that suddenly appears on a beautiful desert island, there can only be one explanation: something from the outside must have brought it in. Maybe an infected bird flew in; maybe a healthy bird flew in and dropped a diseased seed, which then blighted a whole crop. So what 'flew' into the first paradise? Very obviously Satan. Dissatisfaction is first seen in Satan. He didn't get what he wanted and so he has been trying to spread the canker of discontentment ever since. It would seem that even though Satan was one of God's special angels and held a favoured position, it was not enough, he wanted more.

> You said in your heart,
> 'I will ascend to heaven;
> I will raise my throne
> above the stars of God;
> I will sit enthroned on the mount of assembly,
> on the utmost heights of
> the sacred mountain.
> I will ascend above the tops of the clouds;
> I will make myself like the Most High' (Is. 14:13–4).

The text does not say that this is Satan, but along with other references to him in the Bible it has been concluded that Isaiah is describing what Satan tried to do along with an explanation of how this behaviour led to his expulsion from heaven,

> How you have fallen from heaven,
> O morning star, son of the dawn!
> You have been cast down to the earth,
> you who once laid low the nations! (Is. 14:12).

If you think about it, this basic attitude, which says what I have got is not enough, I want more, lies not only at the root of personal unhappiness and discontentment, but also at the root of most crime. It spreads and pollutes. If I don't have and you do have, then I can steal to get what I want, I can cheat to get what I want. If you have taken something from me, then I am entitled to revenge and I can murder you to get my own back. Take a glance through your daily paper and work out how many of the crimes are a direct or even indirect result of discontentment, which leads to greed, which leads to jealousy, which leads to . . . Satan has never changed his strategy, he doesn't need to, it is so successful. And just in case you might be a Christian who is sitting there gloating over the fact that your name has never appeared in the paper and you are immune to all this deplorable type of behaviour, take a look at James' warning:

> What causes fights and quarrels among you? Don't they come from your desires that battle within you? You want something but don't get it. You kill and covet, but you cannot have what you want. You quarrel and fight (Jas. 4:1–2a).

This is written in a letter to God's people, not a national newspaper. God's people have always been taken in by Satan's lies. The Bible is full of dissatisfied women who not only allowed him to whisper in their ear, but also, acted on what they heard, often with disastrous consequences. I am sure there are many disgruntled men too, but they are never quite as free in expressing their feelings and the women make theirs so obvious! Let us look at several of them; women who the woman at the well would have been very familiar with if she had really read her Scriptures. If only she had known it, she was in good company, or was it bad company? You might think your situation is unique, but if you take a good look in the Bible you will find, however surprised you may be by circumstances or events, that others have been there before and nothing shocks God.

Infertility has always been a very hard thing to accept and from the beginning of time women have tried to find ways round it. When Sarai, Abram's wife could not conceive she decided to take matters into her own hands. It is difficult for any couple to face the prospect of being childless, but for a couple in early Bible times it was almost unbearable. Children were seen as an expression of God's blessing and therefore to be without them may well have suggested that the couple were living under his disapproval. Barrenness was thought to be a sign of God's disapproval. Unlike today's couples, Israelites would never ask, 'Shall we have children?' or 'How many children shall we have?' or 'Shall we both have a career for twenty years and then start trying for a family?' They would have discussed children before the wedding and would be keen to have them as soon as possible. God had told them to be fruitful and to multiply and they took their obedience seriously!

If there was ever a problem with having children, the wife would be blamed. She would see it as her fault and therefore her responsibility to put things right. With this in mind Sarai took it upon herself to come up with a solution to their dilemma: she would get her husband to sleep with her maid, Hagar, and the first surrogate baby would be born. Sarai's discontentment led her into nagging her husband and worse than that it led her into persuading him to disobey God.

Beware of ensnaring others in your web of discontent. Sarai of course is wily and clever in her approach. She implies that it is God's fault. Instead of realising that because they are having no children God must obviously want them to wait, she sees the delay as a denial and tells Abram that this is a permanent state of affairs and they need to provide a way out. 'The Lord has kept me from having children. Go sleep with my maid servant; perhaps I can build a family through her' (Gen. 16:2).

This was a very bad suggestion. God had specifically rebuked Abram when he had complained to him about their childlessness, 'You have given me no children; so a servant in my household will be my heir' (Gen.15:3). 'This man will not be your heir,' God had said. Maybe Abram had not told Sarai about this command nor the assurance that God then gave him as he showed him the night sky and promised him that his offspring would be as numerous as the stars he could see. Whether she knew or not, Abram knew that God had not forgotten them, he had plans for them and when his wife came up with suggestions, which were a denial of those plans, he simply gave in: 'Abram agreed to what Sarai said' (Gen.16:2). It is almost comical that when Hagar conceives and starts to despise Sarai, Sarai conveniently forgets it was all her idea and goes and blames Abraham for the fact that she is even more unhappy than she was before! 'You are responsible for the wrong I am suffering,' she says (Gen. 16:5). How often this scenario is worked out in close relationships. Wife is not happy and nags husband who suggests they move to a new house in a new part of town, only to find when she gets there, she does not like the neighbours and now blames him for ever suggesting they went there in the first place!

Sarai's discontentment leads to disobedience. The repercussions were disastrous if not colossal. Hagar, the maid, produced Ishmael who, in time, became the father of the Arab race. There was conflict between Ishmael and Isaac – the son Abram and Sarai eventually had together – from the start and there has been conflict between Jews and Arabs ever since. Two nations locked in hostility towards each other throughout history, thousands dying because of that hostility and in the background one discontented woman, who was not willing to trust God, who was not willing to wait and who therefore unwittingly caused it all. Once the pebble had dropped into the pond the repercussions would ripple on relentlessly.

Not having children may be one reason for dissatisfaction, but so also can not liking the ones you've got! Abraham and Sarah (as they became) had Isaac, who married Rebekah, and together these two had the twins, Jacob and Esau. Rebekah had been through the whole infertility struggle and you would have thought she would have been overjoyed to give birth to two little boys. Maybe she was content with them when they were small, but they were very different in character and temperament and she and her husband made the big mistake of having favourites.

> The boys grew up, and Esau became a skilful hunter, a man of the open country, while Jacob was a quiet man, staying among the tents. Isaac, who had a taste for wild game, loved Esau, but Rebekah loved Jacob (Gen. 25:27).

What a sad statement and how foolish the parents were in their favouritism. Later in the text, Esau is actually referred to as Isaac's son, whereas Jacob is referred to as Rebekah's son. As the first-born, Esau should have inherited his father's birthright, but Rebekah wanted her favourite to get it, so in her discontentment with the situation, she, like Sarah, decided to do a bit of wheeling and dealing. She persuaded Jacob to dress up as Esau and trick his father into giving him the blessing. Once again, the consequences were disastrous. The boys were constantly in conflict and Jacob ended up having to run for his life all because his mother had been unhappy with things as they were and had decided to manipulate circumstances to her own end.

Not all the dissatisfied women of the Bible have problems with children or lack of them, some had problems with their brothers or, to be more accurate, themselves. Miriam, Moses' sister, is a classic example of someone who starts so well as a great example and inspiration to others and yet ends in disgrace. When Moses had led the children of Israel out of Egypt and through the Red Sea, it was Miriam who led the women in praise to God. She 'took a tambourine in her hand, and all the women followed her with tambourines and dancing' (Ex. 15:20). She was probably proud of her brother, but she knew it was all God's doing and as she focused her worship on him, she would no doubt have had a positive influence throughout the camp. But things were soon to change.

A dispute arose within the family. Two's company and three's a crowd and Moses, his brother Aaron, and his sister Miriam had certainly become a crowd. They were unhappy with Moses. They pretended it was because he was married to a Cushite woman, rather than an Israelite, but the root cause of their grumbling against him was really jealousy. They started to snipe at him behind his back. ' "Has the Lord spoken only through Moses?" they asked. "Hasn't he also spoken through us?" And the Lord heard this' (Num. 12:2).

God hears our grumblings! Because Miriam was jealous, she became critical and disloyal and the canker of discontent began to spread. But God would not tolerate this attack on his faithful, humble servant Moses and his 'anger burned against them'. Before she knew it God had given them a good telling off and when Miriam looked down, she was 'leprous, like snow'. Thanks to Moses' pleadings on behalf of his sister, God restricted the punishment to seven days confinement outside the camp before Miriam could be restored. It is very interesting how her bad behaviour, her grumbling and sniping at others because she is personally unhappy, holds everyone else back. 'So Miriam was confined outside the camp for seven days, and the people did not move on till she was brought back' (Num. 12:15). I wonder how many times I have held my family back, or my team of Sunday School teachers, or my work colleagues, because of my personal grumps and gripes? A negative spirit can be so destructive and we are lucky people who have someone to intercede for us with God on our behalf.

It is obvious that when we are out of sorts with ourselves and then others, there is only one solution and it is to acknowledge our own responsibility for the situation and to put things right within ourselves. However, discontentment is a disease and many have been led to believe that the solution does not lie within the individual, it lies out there somewhere. We do not need to confront and face ourselves; we simply need to escape from ourselves. The whole world of advertising is built on the 'If only' myth. I am unhappy with the tedium of cooking, if only I could get a bigger kitchen, with pine cupboards as the lady on the phone offered me last week, then I would be a wonderful cook and we would all sit round the big table as a happy family feasting on the latest sumptuous repast. But we are not a happy family I hear you say! Simple! If only you pop that little beef-flavoured cube in the stew, all quarrelling will cease and harmony will prevail; that's what the advert promises, isn't it?

If only I had a prettier bedroom with fitted wardrobes, I would look like Julia Roberts and my man would look like . . . well whoever, and our love life would be cosmic! Of course it would help if I had just driven up in my sexy little car, with my hair washed in that special shampoo and my latest clothes from Gap, smelling of that fresh new powder that leaves them looking so white. No matter that our marriage is falling apart because we are too busy and no longer trust each other, but pretend we do; we can just get the right products, paper over the cracks and it will all be all right. That's what the neighbours will think anyway. We've always got that luxury holiday coming up, which we booked last Christmas when we were stuck inside in the cold and were really getting on each other's nerves.

If only I could have this. If only I could go there. If only I could taste just a little, said Eve, then I'd be happy, and she did and we have been unhappy ever since. How many of us put up with the present because we believe one day it will change.

Every weekend millions of people buy that magic lottery ticket, their passport to happiness, the fulfilment of all their dreams. I hear them at the supermarket check out, just before they go off to fill in their winning numbers . . .

'How are you doing Joan?'

'Oh, not bad.'

'Its been a long winter hasn't it?'

'Yes and this damp does my rheumatism no good at all. Oh well, Frank says when we win the lottery, we can go and live in Florida.'

'Oh I wouldn't want to do that. I'd miss all my friends. Sam says we're going to get a big house.'

'Oh I'd never do that, Frank would want his mother to come and stay.'

'Ah well, here's your change, see you next week Doris.' We're all the same, so easily tempted into thinking there must be something better for me waiting just round the corner.

Several years ago God challenged me about this very attitude. I was at the doctors yet again with my son and his recurring ear problems. One of my daughters had had the same problems and so I was familiar with the procedure. Painful nights, broken sleep, hang on hoping it will go away, resist antibiotics as long as possible and finally give in, arriving at the doctors desperate for some relief for all of us. I could not wait to hear those words, 'You can come in now Mrs Price.' Our wait would be over, the doctor would provide the solution and everything would be all right, until the next time. As I sat there I sensed God was saying to me, 'Your life is like this. You feel as though you have been here so often, you are practically living in the waiting room. And that is what you are doing: living in the waiting room.' It was true. The children were little and I had begun to feel as though my life was on hold.

I was brought up short. I realised that the only reason I got through the present was because I was hanging on, waiting for things to change. My husband was travelling a lot and I was feeling terribly stuck. I was not teaching, even though I had spent five years training to do so. I was not playing any sport, because it involved Saturday matches and the children needed either looking after or taking to their own activities. I was not thankful for all the wonderful things God had given me. I was marking time and waiting to hear that call: 'You can come in now Mrs Price.' I thought God had this fantastic life and ministry, somewhere just waiting for me to step into and everything else was simply a time filler. Our bedroom desperately needed decorating and I didn't do it, reasoning that it was not worth it, as we would soon be moving on. Seventeen years later, we were still there. I did make new drapes; the bedroom was completely changed and so hopefully was my heart and attitude.

I saw a credit card advert one day which said, 'We'll take the waiting out of wanting.' I would say, in my life, God has taken the wanting out of waiting. There are two lessons I have learned. Firstly, there will always be a restlessness in the human heart which cannot be satisfied outside of God himself. Whatever situation I am in, even if it is not fulfilling in itself, which of course motherhood can and should be, true satisfaction comes from resting in God and in my relationship with him. What the world offers glitters so brightly, but fades so quickly. Of course it is attractive. Who wouldn't want a pretty bedroom, a spacious kitchen and lovely holidays? They are nice things to have, but they will never satisfy that inner hunger for meaning and purpose, which we all know deep within us. 'Everyone who drinks this water will be thirsty again, but whoever drinks the water I give him will never thirst,' Jesus said to the woman at the well and to me. 'Dear woman you are expending an awful lot of energy, getting through the day, but you are dropping your bucket in the wrong well!'

At times our circumstances seem dark and lonely and it is hard to see they have any purpose in themselves. This leads to the second thing I have learnt and am still learning: Sometimes, you just have to hang on and keep trusting. I know some people who have this little poster in a prominent place in their homes.

HERE I AM
SERVING GOD
JUST WHERE GOD WANTS ME TO BE
DOING WHAT GOD WANTS ME TO DO
UNTIL HE TELLS ME TO DO SOMETHING ELSE.

When no one sees or cares what we do most of the time, we can be tempted to think that God also doesn't see and doesn't care. He is out there somewhere; I am stuck here in the waiting room, listening for his call. How far from the truth our thinking has led us. When a seed lies in hard, cold, wintry ground waiting for the spring, it has not been forgotten by the caring gardener. He put it in just the right place, at just the right time, knowing that in several months shoots will appear and then the bright flowers and then the harvest. However, while it lies there, something is happening. The seed case is breaking open, the seed is literally falling into the ground and dying so that the resurrection may happen and it will be raised to new life. Resist the temptation to live your life on the stage. Being famous is a modern obsession, but God's heroes are more often quiet, unseen and unsung. 'We must be careful not to interpret the days of obscurity and isolation as meaningless and unimportant.'[6] Jesus spent thirty years in the shadows before he stepped into the blazing light of God's public purpose. Gladys Aylward, whose story was told in the book, *The Small Woman*, spent years working amongst villagers, hidden in the mountains in China until the Japanese invaded and she marched hundreds of children over the mountains to freedom and to fame. You may never know fame and it is indeed a very dangerous goal to have, but you will have the opportunity to really know God and thereby understand the very purpose for which you were made.

When you are tempted to say to God, 'Oh God I've had enough. I'm tired of living in the waiting room. Please let me out.' Linger long enough you will hear the simple reply, 'No my child, you may not come out yet, but you may let me in.' Jesus is the I AM who makes the present make sense. You may feel suspended between the past and the future, just as the woman at the well did, but if he is present in the present, it will make sense. He is there for you now. To the hungry he says, 'I am the bread of life.' To the thirsty he says, 'I am the living water.' To the lost he says, 'I am the light of the world.' To the lonely he says, 'I am the good shepherd.' To the weak and resourceless he says, 'I am the vine.' To the disillusioned he says, 'I am the way.' To the confused he says, I am the truth.' To the dying he says, 'I am the life.'

Your waiting is over. Your wanting is over. Because I AM.

Chapter 6

Will Jesus Step Out of the Sky One Day?

'When he comes he will explain everything to us . . .'

Having thought about how we deal with the past and the present let us move on in the conversation the Samaritan woman has with Jesus and see what it teaches about our attitude to the future. 'It can only get better,' people say when you are struggling through a hard patch or when the weather is particularly tedious and dull! A belief that up ahead things will improve seems necessary for survival in the most mundane, and in the most dire circumstances. Viktor Frankl in his book, *Man's Search for Meaning*, recorded how during the Second World War people in concentration camps used to envisage the meals they would cook and eat when they were freed and somehow this helped keep them alive. It was not the thought of spaghetti bolognese that gave them a reason to live, it was simply having hope that one day they would actually sit at a table and eat spaghetti which lifted their horizon. All of us have a belief system in place about the future even though we may not have realised it; the woman of Samaria was no exception.

Both Jews and Samaritans believed in a Messiah, a chosen one, who would one day accomplish God's redemptive purpose for his people. For hundreds of years they had waited. The Jews were expecting a king or a strong political figure who would rescue them from whatever power had taken over their land and restore their kingdom. The Samaritan idea was less political and worldly. They were looking for *Hushab*, the Converter or Returning One who would re-establish worship on Gerizim, where they supposed the tabernacle was hidden.[7]

Deep in the psyche of all of us it would seem that we have a need to be rescued. I saw a group of women recoil in horror when that was suggested to them by Cosby during a discussion on *The Cosby Show*. Maybe it was because he provocatively implied it was only women who were waiting to be rescued and not men. Consider the plot underlying most films and indeed classic stories; it is hard to find one that does not include the idea of rescue somewhere: *Lord of the Rings*, *Gone with the Wind*, *Romeo and Juliet*, even *Winnie the Pooh*, who needed Rabbit to rescue him after he ate too much honey and got stuck in Rabbit's hole! Usually the rescuer is another person, who has their flaws, but does the job! This rescuer is only a reflection of the real Saviour who unknowingly we are all waiting to meet for the first time or if we know him, to welcome on his return.

The Samaritan woman was waiting to be rescued although she probably did not realise it. She seems to be getting increasingly confused as she listens to Jesus speak about worship and truth and spirit, but in the midst of it all one repeated phrase stirs a response in her heart. 'A time is coming . . . A time is coming . . .', he says and she bursts in with confidence, 'I know that Messiah is coming . . .'. This is the first time in this conversation that she claims she knows anything. Up to this point she has been all too aware of what she does not know. Not only is she sure he is coming, but she knows what he will do: 'When he comes he will explain everything to us.' He will be someone who tells the truth, someone she can trust. In the midst of all the drudgery and disappointment of everyday life, he is the one glimmer of hope on the horizon.

It is obvious that nothing she has been taught or told up to this point has satisfied her. She is well aware that her understanding is deficient because she is still waiting for explanations. She has picked up a belief system which has left her feeling confused, no doubt condemned and probably very frustrated. Maybe her long string of relationships with men has all been about her deep spiritual longing and nothing to do with being hungry for physical satisfaction as it may superficially appear. Immediate gratification may provide a substitute, but will never provide a solution for the need to know a permanent, enduring love. We can be so quick to judge those who would seem to be promiscuous, without taking the time to look deeper and see the real need for love, acceptance, worth, compassion and above all significance, which were about to be realised for this woman as she looked into the face of the ultimate rescuer and the only saviour and heard him say, 'I who speak to you am he.'

The one who was a distant hope, a long way off in the future somewhere, has stepped into her present and life as she knows it is over. She leaves her water jar, steps out of the shadowlands and sets off to tell the world she has looked into the face of the sun and lived! The waiting is over. The wanting has passed. She has been rescued from herself, her sin and her circumstances, and all she wants to do is bring light into the darkness of all those who have been fumbling around in the shadows with her, calling it life and probably calling her names! But wait a moment, we are running ahead! Before this can happen she has had to face the fact that her concept of the Messiah of the 'then' did not affect her world in the 'now'.

So how about you? How does your perspective on the future affect the way you live now? Do you wish the future and all it holds could step into your present and sit on your well or are you frightened of what lies up ahead and hope that it won't happen for a long time. What are you sure of? What do you fear? Of course the future can mean many things. It may mean the immediate future – tomorrow when you are meeting an old friend or going for a job interview – or it may mean something huge and apocalyptic at the end of history. In the seventies a survey was conducted in secondary schools all over the UK and the students were asked to list their biggest fears. Two things emerged at the top of the majority of lists: world destruction through nuclear war and the break up of parents. One international and political, the other domestic and personal. Both equally frightening and both menacingly out there in the future waiting to happen and all the more threatening because they were beyond the control of each teenager who felt like a victim in waiting. Does the fact that one day the Messiah sat down on a well in Samaria have any bearing on the way we see both the immediate and the distant future? I believe it does.

Does God want us to know what lies ahead? Are there some things we are allowed to know and some things we aren't? We have been told Jesus is coming back, but we have not been told when. In fact 'No one knows about that day or hour, not even the angels in heaven, nor the Son, but only the Father' (Mt. 24:36). We are not to concern ourselves with when he is coming, but with what we are doing in the meantime, which is much more straightforward. 'Therefore keep watch, because you do not know the day or the hour' (Mt. 25:13). We are to be ready.

I remember visiting Queen Elizabeth's beautiful residence at Balmoral in Scotland. We had not dropped in for tea with the Queen as many people seem to think the English make a habit of doing, but to look round as much of the house and the gardens as they would allow us while she was not in residence. We saw a luxurious ballroom, a sumptuous dining room and a few other showcase rooms in the main building and then I was keen to look around the gardens. What a disappointment! The main beds near the house were bare and as I wandered behind hedges and round near the green houses I was simultaneously dismayed and reassured to discover she had more weeds than I had in my little garden back home! The reason was that they simply were not expecting the Queen. When they knew she was coming, they would make everything spic and span. It's easy to lose heart hanging on waiting for someone to come and allow weeds to grow all around us. I know a lot of young people who think that God is down the track at the end of old age somewhere and not worth considering until arthritis sets in and there is nothing else to do but sit around and think. Death is not confined to old people and can come very suddenly. Cushioning ourselves with life insurance policies may give us some sense of control and protection over the future but in reality a visit from the Saviour in the now and a willingness to be rescued in the present is the only way we can be assured of the future.

For many people, thoughts about the future include vague notions about heaven. We are assured of Heaven, it is a real place and we know how to go there but what will it really be like? There are certain questions we can already answer. Here are one or two pointers:

Do I already have anything in heaven?
Yes!
Treasures that won't rust (Mt. 6:20).
My name (Lk. 10:20).
A place prepared for me (Jn. 14:2).
An eternal building (2 Cor. 5:1).

Who will be there?
Thousands of people (Dan. 7:10).
People from every nation (Lk. 13:29).
Those who are properly dressed! (Rev. 22:14).
Thousands of angels (Rev. 5:11).

Will I be me?
Yes, but with a new body! (Phil. 3:21).

What will we do?
Enjoy a life of . . .
Fellowship (Jn. 14:3),

Rest (Rev. 14:13),
Knowledge (1 Cor. 13:12),
Holiness (Rev. 21:27),
Joy (Rev. 21:40),
Service (Rev. 22:3),
Abundance (Rev. 21:6),
Glory (Col. 3:4),
Worship (Rev. 7:9–12).

What will not be there?
Hunger, thirst and drought (Rev. 7:16),
Sea (Rev. 21:1),
Sorrow, crying and pain (Rev. 21:4),
Curse (Rev. 22:3),
Night (Rev. 22:5),
Death (Rev. 21:4).

These pictures, given in the Bible, are exciting and at the same time confusing. The images used are fantastical and dream-like and provoke our curiosity as much as they provide comfort. A friend told me how her son had been very upset one day and when she asked him what the matter was he said he was really worried because he had worked out that because she was older than he was, she would probably go to heaven first. She agreed. He then went on to tell her his real concern. 'Heaven is so big,' he sobbed. 'How will I find you?' Putting her arm round him she reassured him, 'When I get to heaven I'll save you a seat!' How wonderful. It is so much easier to walk into a crowded room, in a strange place when you know your friend, who has been there before, has promised to save you a seat and will be there, waiting and waving.

As I said earlier, when I was a child I often asked if anyone had been to heaven and come back to tell us about it. I was looking for reassurance. No one told me at the time but later I discovered that Jesus actually gave it.

> Do not let your hearts be troubled. Trust in God; trust also in me. In my Father's house are many rooms; if it were not so, I would have told you so. I am going there to prepare a place for you. And if I go and prepare a place for you, I will come back and take you to be with me that you also may be where I am (Jn. 14:1–3).

Not only will he have everything ready, but he will come and be our personal escort to the place he has prepared. I find this a very comforting thought when I am at a funeral and my mind starts thinking about where that person is now. I know only their body is in the coffin, but the real them, the part of them which will be alive for ever is being taken, maybe even by the hand, to a wonderful place far beyond their wildest imaginings. And Jesus is there every step of the way – you won't get lost and you will arrive on time! Yesterday a friend came round to my house and picked me up in her truck to take me out to lunch to a place where she had already booked a table. All I had to do was get in and enjoy the ride! I am new to this area and I usually set off, in plenty of time and with map in hand, just hoping I will not miss the right exit off the freeway and wishing I had remembered my glasses because I can't read all those small road names! How relaxed I felt waiting to be picked up, not even knowing where we were going, never mind how to get there, but confident that she did.

I remember getting a phone call some time ago which made me increasingly irritated. As it progressed I found myself answering questions that were really nobody's business, and certainly not the business of a complete stranger. To make matters worse it was dinner time, which is when phone sales people always know you will be in. It went something like this:

'Are you between 18 and 85?'
'Yes.'
'Do you or your husband have full-time employment?'
'Yes.'
'You might be a prize winner.'

(Cynical silent pause from me!)
'Are you a home owner?'
'No.'
(Rude silent pause from her!)
'Oh well in that case this is not relevant for you ...
Goodbye!'
(Bang. Down went the phone – her's and mine!)

Charming! Obviously I was not qualified for whatever they were going to offer because I did not have the financial security that owning a home would suggest. I wish I had been less touchy and much quicker off the mark in seeing an opportunity for God rather than a chance to nurse my wounded pride and get off the phone as quickly as possible. I wish I had said, 'But I do have a home; it's in heaven; it's safe and secure; Jesus is preparing it right now; and one day he is going to take me there even if I am under eighteen or over eighty-five. Do you have a home in heaven? Would you like to know how you can?' Ah well, next time . . .

You might be thinking, at this point, that it is all very well to be confident about the Messiah coming, as the Samaritan woman was, and to be sure about my home in heaven, as Paul was (2 Cor. 5:1), but what about the more immediate future? I can trust God for my ultimate destination and for his return one day, but what about tomorrow? Do I trust God for tomorrow, for next week, for next year? 'Can you see Thursday?' my son Matthew asked me one day. 'No it's something we can't look at,' I replied. "Can Jesus see Thursday?' he persisted and I was glad to be able to reassure him that although I am very limited, he isn't: 'Yes, he can see Thursday and all your Thursdays,' I said.

People have been wanting to peep into the future since the beginning of time. Horoscopes are the first page many turn to as they open a newspaper, keen to know what their stars say and what they might expect in their lives. Predictions are often seized upon and then when the date arrives and the certain event does not happen people feel angry and let down. Several predicted that the last total eclipse in Britain would herald the end of time. It came and went. The sky darkened, the birds stopped singing, time was suspended in an eerie silence, people held their breath, and then it passed. The sun came out, the birds started to sing again and a huge crowd gathered outside a bookshop in France demanding their money back on a book predicting the end of time that had sold very well in the previous few weeks. I am sure the owners were still in the dark, huddled behind tightly drawn blinds and carefully locked doors. The protesters wanted someone to blame. No doubt the author had long gone, probably on a wonderful holiday funded by all his royalties and it is rather hard to blame God for something he didn't do, when he had never actually said he would! I wonder if fortune-tellers can actually be sued when the things they saw in their crystal ball don't materialise! No doubt their insurance premium is astronomical!

And what does God think of it all? It would seem he mocks the profession because even if they could manage to guess correctly about the future they are powerless to do anything about it. 'Let the astrologers come forward, those stargazers who make predictions month by month. Let them save you from what is coming' (Is. 47:13). Involvement in such a dangerous and ultimately futile pursuit is forbidden: 'Let no one be found among you who practises divination' (Deut. 18:18).

Of course, that does not mean God does not recognise the hungry heart and seeking soul who may well be simply searching in the wrong place. It was through astrology that the wise men were led to Jesus. I am challenged to recognise what could well be a search for God rather than a defiance of him and to pray for those I know who use tarot cards and for the palm reader whose bright lights on the shop, at the end of my road, are deliberately designed to entice fellow seekers who have lost their way on their journey through life and are desperate for any sense of direction that may be offered.

You may at this point be feeling pretty smug as you read about some people's need to try and predict the future. 'Heaven forbid!' you say, '(and it does so I am OK!). I would never visit a fortune-teller or try and predict what is going to happen.' Oh no? Don't you sometimes open your Bible and just hope you will see that verse which will reassure you that you should move to a certain place, there is no danger up ahead, your sickness will be cured, etc.? No doubt God does speak very clearly and specifically through his written word, but he speaks in the context of prayer and a relationship, not as you land your finger on any old page, trusting that this game of verse lottery is bound to come up with something and you will keep on pointing and then opening your eyes until it does or at least until you find what you are looking for! I know, I have done it!

Something else I have done, which maybe more people would be willing to admit to, is not necessarily to try and predict the future, but to imagine myself into it: imagine all the changes up ahead; imagine if this happens to my child; or if my parent becomes ill and I am too far away to help. This too is forbidden in the Bible because it is another human strategy for coping with the uncertainties of tomorrow rather than trusting God. It is commonly known as worry!

> 'Do not worry about your life, what you will eat or drink or about your body, what you will wear . . . Who of you by worrying can add a single hour to your life? . . . do not worry about tomorrow, for tomorrow will worry about itself. Each day has enough trouble of its own' (Mt. 6:25, 27, 34).

Jesus was not dismissing our concerns, or indeed negating them, he was simply saying you need to prioritise. When you realise that your needs are God's priority, he feeds the birds and clothes the fields with lilies and you are much more valuable than they are, then all you need to do is 'seek first his kingdom and his righteousness, and all these things will be given to you as well' (Mt. 6:33). Because you are at the top of God's priority list, you can relax and he and his purposes can be at the top of yours, rather than you and your purposes.

Paul also takes up the same theme when he says, 'The Lord is near. Do not be anxious about anything, but in everything, by prayer and petition, with thanksgiving, present your requests to God' (Phil. 4:6). You have concerns, there are requests to be made: so make them! Don't hug them to yourself, feeling you shouldn't have them at all and if you sort them all out by yourself maybe God will never get to know! God is not waiting to rebuke us because we have worries, he is waiting to catch them all when we fling them in his direction. 'Cast all your anxiety on him,' Peter says, going on to give a very good reason, 'because he cares for you' (1 Pet. 5:7). There is nothing worse than sharing your worries with someone who doesn't really seem to be listening and who therefore doesn't seem to care. God does care and will not take refuge behind the newspaper while you pour out all your troubles; you see, he has never had a hard day at the office and is only to willing to be your burden-bearer!

And now we are on the subject of husbands (you mean you didn't notice?!), the reason I have had to deal with the whole issue of worry is because I was a terrible worrier and I married a man who wasn't. Refusing to believe it was just a male/female thing I have thought long and hard about why I (and therefore I can assume a lot of other people), worry. Again I think the way we view the more distant and the immediate future comes into play here. We can know and really believe that 'the Lord is good and his love endures for ever, His faithfulness through all generations' (Ps. 100:5). We can have a certainty that stretches down the years; but does it stretch back towards my world and next week? We can know the theory but be robbed of the pleasure, adventure, peace, reassurance, confidence, hope and joy that his faithfulness brings by that little weasel, worry.

At first I thought I worried because I was weak and then I realised I worried because I was trying to be too strong. I would look at any given situation that concerned me, that I knew I could do nothing about, and sitting on the sidelines I would feel helpless. I had to do something. Consequently, I worried. 'Worry is like a rocking chair,' a young student told me, 'it gives you something to do but it gets you nowhere.' How true, I thought. Is she talking about herself or her observations of me! Whatever, she is telling the truth. I have rocked backwards and forwards in that chair until the floor has begun to wear out beneath me. I finally get up. I have done something. I have tired myself out, annoyed the people around me, ruined my carpet and worst of all, left God out. 'Cast your cares upon me,' he's been saying. I can see his lips moving but I can't hear the words because my squeaky rocker needs oiling and because of the noise of all the other rockers lined up around me, rocking to the same rhythm:

I'm so worried, there's nothing I can do,
But that's OK 'cause you're worried too.
The children, the parents, the bills to pay,
I'm so busy worrying,
There's no time to pray!

Worry can have a paralysing effect. The dictionary definition is 'to be unduly concerned' and the word comes from the German word, *wurgen*, to strangle or choke. When you are really worrying about something it is hard to think clearly about anything else. It can be overwhelming as it dictates how you feel and therefore how you act. I have found that worry is all-invasive. It harasses you mentally, winds you up emotionally, tenses you up physically and strangles you spiritually until you are left feeling you are gasping for air and seeking some way of escape. Some people have the sort of mind in which they can compartmentalise their lives and thoughts into cupboards. They can open and shut the cupboard doors as they please, dealing with the contents of that cupboard or simply shutting it away to be dealt with later. I do not have that sort of mind. I try and put things in the 'Things of concern to think about later' cupboard, shut the door firmly behind me and rush out to get on with something else in my life. I am in the car, I am walking round the shops, I am hiking up a hill, I am playing tennis and, lo and behold, I am still besieged by the contents! They are whizzing round the car as I pause at the lights, they are laughing at me in the supermarket as I try and focus on something for dinner that night, they are clouding the view as I pause for breath on the mountain, they are my reason for hitting the ball into the net for the third time because I cannot concentrate. They are choking me because I am unduly concerned and I am insisting on bearing my own burdens.

Finding myself in this unhappy state of mind I asked myself two very obvious questions: What do I worry about and why do I worry? The first one was easy to answer. I worry about (not necessarily in this order) my husband's health, my children's safety and schooling, my parents, my family, my friends, myself. I am sure you can complete the list. By the way, if you can't, and are tempted to jump ship at this point because you cannot identify with this sort of worrying, I would encourage you to read on because even if you are not a worrier you no doubt know one and instead of them being an irritant and frustration to you, a little understanding may enable you to be a help to them.

When I dealt with the next question, Why do I worry?, I was about to pat myself on the back; 'I worry because I care,' I proudly announced to myself. 'I worry because I love people,' I declared, a sanctimonious smile spreading across my face and then I heard it. A very faint, but very firm whisper; 'Do I not care? Do I not love them all, may I suggest even more than you do?' Silence. My heart was exposed. 'OK, God. The truth is I am a controlling person. The future and all that is going to happen to all of us is something I can't control, so I worry.' When God holds a mirror up, it is not so he can gloat over the spots we both see there, but so we can acknowledge the problem and do something about it.

I was reminded that unless we become like little children we cannot enter the kingdom of heaven. I was being far too grown up and responsible with my worries. I thought about my own children and whether they had been worriers. They worried more the older they got, the more independent they became of us, their parents, and the more they took on themselves. When they were very little they simply did not worry. They lived in the present. They accepted the present and worked within it, rather than constantly working out how they may change what was happening so it would be better in the future. They trusted their mum and dad because as long as they were around they were safe and they always knew someone bigger than them was in control. I have a friend whose little girl woke up one day and asked, 'Is it today or tomorrow?' In a sense it didn't matter because her mum would be in both, so everything would be OK. We had a cassette that we played often in the car when the children were little. I still remember one of the lines and I hope they do too! 'Today is the tomorrow you worried about yesterday and all is well,' the little voice sang out. That does not mean that all is perfect or fantastic or even exciting; what is well about it is that God is still in his heaven and I am on earth and he cares for me. That may sound simple, but our relationship with our heavenly father should be simple. In our earthly relationship with our parents we gauge our maturity level by how dependent we still are on mum and dad. Our whole upbringing, if it is a healthy one, is designed to lead up gradually towards independence when we can confidently fly the nest and live on our own. In our relationship with God exactly the opposite needs to happen: the more we mature, the more we depend on him, the more we become like little children, looking to him for our every need, in fact our every breath.

Some may say that the reason children find it easier to trust is because they do not see the big picture. They do not have the experience to predict the dangers ahead and so they have no need to worry. My son and I learnt to ski a few weeks ago. As we progressed from the beginners' hill to the green slope I felt my anxiety level rise. He did not! With great confidence he was off, whizzing down the slopes and patiently waiting for me at the bottom. Where was I? At the top, weighing up all the pros and cons, thinking about all the people I knew who had broken bones doing the very thing I was about to do, realising this was only the beginning – once I got down this slope I would then have to master the chair lift to get back up! I had reason to worry, I told myself, as I launched off trying to clutch my misgivings to my chest but realising I couldn't ski if I clutched anything to my chest! I let go and enjoyed the ride. 'Usually it is mum who is proud of me,' Matthew told Charles that night, 'but today I was so proud of her! You should have seen her dad, she just set off and flew down the slopes!' I felt ten-feet tall. If only he had known; that was maybe how it looked from the outside, but it certainly wasn't how it felt on the inside!

The reason I am willing to hurl myself towards possible death and probable injury (sorry but it did feel that dramatic) is because I have learned a wonderful lesson about worry and how we approach things that lie ahead in the future. As I grappled with this whole issue I realised something very obvious. God never promised things would work out, but he did promise he would be there. When I have been going through very difficult times and have not been sure what was going to happen, I have had very well meaning friends who have drawn alongside and said, 'It will be fine, don't worry.' As they have walked away, I have been thankful for their love, but not their counsel. What if it is not fine? Then do I worry? 'No,' said Jesus. In fact he said just the opposite, 'It won't be fine, but don't worry.'

Jesus is utterly realistic as he prepares his disciples for the future. He told them not to worry about the little things, the immediate needs, like food and clothes, as we saw earlier, later he talks about the big things that lie in wait and amazingly he still says, 'Don't worry.' 'When they arrest you, do not worry about what to say or how to say it. At that time you will be given what to say' (Mt. 10:19). He doesn't say, 'Don't worry about whether or not you'll get arrested,' but *'when* they arrest you . . . '. He is telling them how things are going to be, what inevitable dangers they will face and having ascertained the facts he then says, 'Don't worry.' Jesus' message is consistent throughout his ministry. He never pulls any punches, but boldly states, 'In this world you will have trouble' (Jn. 16:33). Why was he so forthright with his disciples? He wanted them to be realistic about life, to know what to expect and therefore not to panic when the tough times came; but more than that, he wanted them to trust him. As soon as he had told them they would face trouble in the world, he went on to shoulder all the responsibility: 'But take heart I have overcome the world.' This is not your battle; it is mine. I am the overcomer, so you don't need to be; you just need to live in the good of what I have done. 'Do not let your hearts be troubled. Trust in God, trust also in me' (Jn. 14:1).

This was not a new idea Jesus had trumped up. God had told his people throughout the Old Testament that when things were tough, he would always be there. 'When [*not if*] you pass through the waters, I will be with you; and when [*not if*] you pass through the rivers; they will not sweep over you. When [*not if*] you walk through the fire, you will not be burned; the flames will not set you ablaze' (Is. 43:2). Once the children of Israel had been released from captivity in Egypt they were constantly mumbling and grumbling in the desert. The journey was much harder and longer than they had expected and so they turned on God and Moses and held them responsible. If your expectations of your walk with God are unrealistic, then when things don't seem to go according to plan it is so easy to become frustrated, angry, disappointed and defeated. But who gave you that plan? Was it some misguided evangelist who told you that if you come to Jesus all your troubles would be over? To be brutally honest and faithful to Jesus' words they are only just beginning! Once you back your truck up behind his (as I once heard a biker say!) you had better be ready for the ride of your life. There are three things, as you face the future, that you can be sure of: pressure, his presence and his protection. As Moses struggled with the overwhelming task of leading thousands of people through hostile territory to an unknown land, he went to God for reassurance: 'If I have found favour in your eyes, teach me your ways so I may know you and continue to find favour with you. Remember that this nation is your people' (Ex. 33:13). In other words, 'I can't take a step further without you God. I can't do this by myself. This is your problem. Without you I can't go on.' 'The Lord replied, 'My Presence will go with you, and I will give you rest' (Ex. 33:14). It is so simple and we have made it so complicated.

Children see it all so clearly as this little conversation I had one day with Matthew shows:

'Will Jesus step out of the sky one day?'

'Yes.'

'Will I see him?'

'Yes. Everyone will see him.'

'When he comes I'm going to climb up and give him a hug. You'll probably have to climb up too because he is so big.'

The Messiah is not simply a distant figure we are all hoping will come one day, he has come, by his Spirit he is here now, and when he comes again, physically, it will be for the second time. He has already stepped from eternity into time, from the future into the present and he will lead us through each day and each tomorrow until the rescue is complete and we arrive safely in heaven. 'I give them eternal life, and they shall never perish; no one can snatch them out of my hand' (Jn. 10:28).

If the woman at the well had lived in our day and age her encounter with Jesus would have been rather like a person watching the television with no thought of ever meeting the people behind the glass screen, but just being content to think about them and switch them on and off at whim. Then one day one of the people actually steps through the screen and comes to sit on your settee, in your living room, to talk to you.

'Religion is not a matter of learning how to think about God but of actually encountering him.'[8] As the Samaritan woman saw that hand outstretched and realised all she had ever longed for had come to meet her, to sit on her well, in her world, she had a simple choice to make. She could put the pot down and take his hand or she could stay right where she was and just hang on . . . hoping that one day this vague Messiah figure would turn up and sort everything out. She decided to trust her eyes and ears, leave her pot and set off. She had had many new beginnings in her life, but maybe this one would actually lead somewhere.

Chapter 7

Up Close and Personal

'. . . his worshippers must worship in spirit and truth.'

Before we go rushing off with the Samaritan woman to see what happens when she tells her neighbours about the remarkable person she has just met, we need to look carefully at some of the issues Jesus raised with her. As he moves in on her private, but in actual fact probably very public life, she tries to sidetrack him by talking about church! Has anyone ever done that with you? Just when you are talking about need and hunger and thirst, usually your own, you hear, 'Yes I go to church. It's so nice. I especially like the candles at Christmas and the cute little play the children do. I was brought up a Catholic.' If she can just let him know that she knows where to meet God then perhaps she won't actually have to!

'Our fathers worshipped on this mountain', she asserts confidently and then goes on to show how broadminded she is. She is aware of all the options. She knows people who go to the Pentecostal down the road and she has neighbours who are Anglicans, 'but you Jews claim that the place where we must worship is in Jerusalem' (Jn. 4:20). Jesus picks up what she says and runs with it, responding with some very straight talking on where we worship, who we worship and how we worship. 'Believe me, woman, a time is coming when you will worship the Father neither on this mountain nor in Jerusalem' (Jn. 4:21). She thinks religion is all about going to a certain place, when, as he is showing her, it is all about encountering a real person. How had she, along with millions of others, got it so wrong? Before we explore her confusion over the *who* and *how* of worship let us go back to the beginning and root out the cause of such a comprehensive and far reaching deception concerning the *where* of worship. Why do people think God is someone we visit in church on a Sunday or someone we pray to over and over again as we kneel on our prayer mat which has to be facing in a particular direction?

When I began to search for God in my summer break, after my first year at university, I was working as a barmaid in a local pub. I had many questions and much pain and so I started calling in at the twelfth-century church I had to pass on my way to work to talk to God. I even took a woman with me who drank far too much and was also very unhappy. There we knelt. I am not sure what we were waiting for but it never happened, not for me anyway. I would be pulling pints an hour later thinking, 'I don't know where God is, but he certainly isn't in that old building. I realise it is beautiful and sacred to many people; for years, generations have come there to find, renew and strengthen their faith, but from where I am, presumably on the outside, I just don't get it. Was that a double gin and tonic you wanted?' No wonder the woman didn't recognise God when he got up close and personal. God didn't do this; he didn't sit on wells and chat with sinners in the noon day sun. He lived far away, beyond the sun or among some fusty old relics in a temple somewhere. God was unreachable and God was certainly untouchable or was he?

At the beginning of time God was very close and very personal, and then something happened. I want to trace God's attempts to stay close to the people he had created to know and love him, and the different ways in which they dealt with his nearness. At first, he never had to introduce himself, as Jesus had to with the Samaritan woman, saying, 'I who speak to you am he.' The first man and woman knew him. He created Adam out of the dust of the ground and breathed into his nostrils the breath of life. I have never had anyone breathe into my nostrils and I never want to because it would probably mean I had been dragged out of a pool or a river and was cold and blue! Or I was a horse and the horse whisperer was trying to calm me down! Breath on your face and indeed up your nostrils is very intimate.

God talked often to Adam but I suggest he visited him rather than dwelt with him. He made Eve because it was not good for Adam to be alone. If God had been there all the time, Adam would not have been alone. He came close, making a garden and not sending him to it but actually putting him in it. He made animals and brought them to the man to name. Since then little children have held up their plasticine models and their splodgy paintings saying, 'Look what I made Daddy', and they have all simply been a copy of what God made and paraded before Adam saying, 'Look what I made.' 'Wow! That is beautiful!' is still the response.

God gave Adam and Eve everything except access to the tree of knowledge of good and evil and, with a little prompting from a slippery snake, that, they realised, was the one thing they wanted more than anything. God was holding out on them. It didn't cross their minds that he was protecting them once they had decided he was preventing them having a pleasurable experience. Surely the consequences of just one little taste of that fruit couldn't be that bad and what was bad anyway? Surely bad wasn't really bad. 'Just do it!' The now is what matters, that moment of pleasure; hang the consequences. So they took and ate and the consequences have hung them and all of us who followed ever since!

Was God still close? He tried to be, but they were hiding. The relationship had changed and for the first time humans knew what it was to be ashamed of themselves and afraid of God. They tried to hide behind a few leaves to cover their nakedness, but when God came close that wasn't enough and so they huddled among the trees.

Then the man and his wife heard the sound of the Lord God as he was walking in the garden in the cool of the day and they hid from the Lord God among the trees of the garden. But the Lord God called to the man, 'Where are you?' He answered, 'I heard you in the garden and I was afraid because I was naked; so I hid' (Gen. 3:8–10).

Feeling exposed and humiliated, when God questioned them about what had happened, they both resorted to blaming someone or something else. 'It was her ... it was the snake ... it was anyone but me ...' They hid behind self-justification; on the attack because they were actually on the defensive. A distance between an intimate couple and between the couple and their God had been established. Now that they had accessed the tree of knowledge of good and evil it would be too painful to live forever, with that knowledge, so out of kindness, he barred their access to the tree of life. They were banished from the garden and we have all lived outside Eden ever since – fighting with each other and fumbling around without God. Sometimes we catch the smell of honeysuckle on a beautiful summer evening, the scent of Eden, something inside us stirs, but before we can follow the yearning of our hearts, we refocus back on the immediate. We gather up the children who are romping through the hedgerows and hurry them home for bath time and bed. It's strange, there it is again, when we read that bedtime story all about Never Never Land, the place where you never grow up, where Peter Pan is the hero, again our heart stirs ... if only it could be true ... if only there was such a place, but this is make believe and we are too grown up for make believe now. Besides there are still the dishes to wash from dinner.

We live in the now, we don't necessarily like it but it is home and it's all we think we've ever known, so we must stay there. 'Where are you?' God still asks. If we were honest we would have to say like Adam, 'I am hiding.' But we don't because we have never let God get close and personal and if he is out there anywhere, we are not sure if we can trust him. We have never been personally introduced to him, we have only heard about him and we are not sure we like what we have heard. We tuck the children in, say or 'do' a prayer without ever actually praying and wander downstairs to watch the TV news tell of countries in turmoil, families in trauma and a world which never stops to ask, 'How did we get into this mess? Was it ever different? Could it ever be different? Most of the wars seem to be over religion anyway. Let's leave it with the politicians, they will keep patching it up, it's not my responsibility. I'm tired and I'm off to bed.'

The religions practised throughout the world seem to be all about striving to please a God we are afraid of and just hoping somehow that we will reach him with our devotion and offerings and he will hear our prayers, but without any real expectation of him actually answering them. They are about turning up at the right place and doing our duty and hoping God will be impressed enough to let us back into that perfect place – then known as Eden, now known as heaven or Paradise or whatever. They are about meditating ourselves into a state of perfection and being projected onto a higher plain. They are about striving to do our best in this life so that in the next one I won't come back as a parasite on some hippopotamus's behind. Here the Bible parts company with all other mainstream religions. The God of the Bible, and therefore Christianity, is not about us striving to reach God but about him constantly reaching to us; asking us where we are, longing to give us a second chance and ultimately laying down his life for us to bring us back to him so that one day, my son Matthew and all of us, can sit on his knee and the closeness will be restored.

The journey back towards what was lost in the garden has been a long hard one for God and we are not there yet. In Jesus, he finally came to live among us and until that baby opened his eyes in a stable two thousand years ago, everything God did on earth prepared for and pointed to his coming. How did people view God in the meantime? Did they ever see him or hear him? Did they look for him or did he always have to go looking for them? How did the gap get so wide and when did they start thinking, like the Samaritan woman and like me, that they had to go to a building or a particular place in order to worship? It's time to take a journey back through the Old Testament, which is where she would have cobbled together her ideas from, and to realise it is not so dark and full of cobwebs as we thought it was.

'Like father like son' the saying goes and in the generations which followed Adam and Eve we sadly find this pattern of sin and shame constantly repeating itself. Just as the first couple did something wrong and then tried to hide, so did one of their children, except he went one step further. When God looked with favour on Abel's sacrifice but was displeased with Cain's, Cain was displeased with God, and feeling jealous and hurt, he killed his brother. Given the chance to tell the truth when questioned about his whereabouts, Cain chose to hide behind lying: 'Then the Lord said to Cain, "Where is your brother Abel?" "I don't know," he replied. "Am I my brother's keeper?" ' (Gen. 14:9).

That cynical, almost insolent, little question hovers above our society. 'Yes' I am sure God wanted to answer, 'You are your brother's keeper. I wanted you to look after him. I put men and women in pairs to do just that. I put children in families to care for each other. Yours was the first family, the beginning of the first society and you murdered your brother. Years later children will murder parents. Fathers will abuse their little daughters. Sons will become missing persons choosing to live on the streets rather than in their family home and you Cain will be the first, 'You will be a restless wanderer on the earth' (Gen. 4:12). Whereas Adam and Eve were driven out of the Garden, Cain actually 'went out from the Lord's presence' and interestingly became the first person to build a city. How many people find refuge in a city when their personal relationships have broken down? Cities are large, busy and anonymous – great places to hide from anyone you choose and especially from God!

But all was not so bleak. God gave Adam and Eve a son, Seth, in the place of Abel and 'At that time men began to call on the name of the Lord' (Gen. 4:25). Here is the beginning of the religious pattern of men reaching, striving, calling to God and for the most part, not listening to a word he was saying. God had made a beautiful world yet within a few generations its inhabitants had wrecked it and God concluded it was time to start again.

> The Lord saw how great man's wickedness on the earth had become, and that every inclination of the thoughts of his heart was only evil all the time. The Lord was grieved that he had made man on the earth, and his heart was filled with pain. So the Lord said, 'I will wipe mankind, whom I have created, from the face of the earth . . . for I am grieved that I have made them' (Gen. 6:6–7).

It seems pretty harsh but this little extract reminds us that it was God's prerogative to do as he pleased. Just in case you think you are in control this is mankind, 'whom I have created'. I am not giving up, but it is time to start again.

There was still no building in sight, but after the flood and the washing of the world, we see the first bricks being piled on top of each other as the sacrificial system is put in place. After weeks of being cooped up with the animals in the ark, after feeding them and cleaning them out Noah could well have been a little protective of his 'pets' but no, as soon as he gets out into the fresh air he sacrifices some of them to God. Why would he do this? Why is it that sacrifice is an integral part of the most primitive religious systems? Did Noah understand that 'without the shedding of blood there is no forgiveness of sins' (as God would later explain to Moses) or did he just respond to a longing in his heart to try and give something to God to show how much he loved him? Maybe Noah had been told the story of the Fall in the Garden and how God himself had shown the way by killing some of the precious animals he had made and using their skin to cover the naked shame of the people he had created. The first blood had been shed by God himself and in the end he would shed his own blood to make the final sacrifice that would take away, cover for ever, the sins of the whole world.

But let's not rush ahead, before that old wooden cross on a hill would bridge the gap between earth and heaven, people would constantly reach upward trying to restore the relationship that had once been so close. After the first altar, came the first and probably the last tower built to reach heaven. The tower of Babel was not built as a sacrifice to God but as a challenge to him. It was an individual's way of saying, 'We don't need God to reach down to us, we can reach up to the heavens all by ourselves and when we do, the whole world will be impressed.'

'Come let us build ourselves a city, with a tower that reaches to the heavens, so that we may make a name for ourselves and not be scattered over the face of the whole earth' (Gen. 11:4). God had specifically told people to 'be fruitful and increase in number; multiply on the earth and increase upon it' and here they were huddling together and building upward instead of outward. Here is man hiding again, this time in his own ability and strength, and here again is God taking the initiative, reaching down to bridge the gap, 'But the Lord came down to see the city and the tower that the men were building. . . . "Come, let us go down . . . " ', he said. The movement is still from there to here, from heaven to earth.

People are now scattered over the whole earth. God still wants contact with his creation so he puts another plan in place. He will choose one particular race and bless them. Not so they can sit around feeling special and pleased with themselves, while everyone else feels left out and not special, but so that the whole world may see how wonderful it is to have a close relationship with a loving heavenly father and may want it for themselves.

I will make you into a great nation
and I will bless you:
I will make your name great,
and you will be a blessing.
I will bless those who bless you,
and whoever curses you I will curse;
and all peoples on earth
will be blessed through you (Gen. 12:2–3).

The Hebrew race would be a huge visual aid to show the world what it was like for people to have that close, intimate relationship with God that they had not known since they left the Garden. He would speak with them, eat with them, meet with them, guide them and once again be up close and personal. Well, he would try . . .

The word of the Lord becomes almost commonplace. The Bible gives no explanation as to how people heard it, but whether or not it was actually an audible voice or just something in their heads, it was loud and clear. The main problem seems to lie not in hearing but in obeying what they heard. God did not speak to vast crowds, but rather to individuals . . . and he still does. Vast crowds may hear, but in those vast crowds it is only certain individuals who respond, reaching back in response to God reaching to them and allowing him to make the connection. Hundreds heard the sermon on the mount; hundreds did not become disciples. Only those who allowed God to get close and personal put their trust in him.

Abraham was chosen to be the father of the Hebrew race. Despite several setbacks, God continues to visit him, speak with him and carry out his plans through him. Our purpose here is not to examine God's relationship with each of his servants but simply to establish that he had one. He forgave them, wrestled with them, rebuked them, responded to their requests and all in all behaved as any father who is committed to his children would. They were often weak, deceitful, disloyal and plainly disobedient but he did not give up and even when all seemed lost and the whole nation found itself imprisoned in Egypt, threatened by a dictator and his false gods, the real God was still in the rescue business.

The faithful few were still endeavouring to reach God and keep the channels of communication open through sacrifice. Indeed it was over the whole issue of freedom to sacrifice as they wanted, that Moses found himself in a head-on conflict with the Pharaoh of the time. In fear and trepidation he went before him, with God's words ringing in his ears, 'say to him, "The Lord, the God of the Hebrews, has sent me to say to you: Let my people go, so that they may worship me in the desert. . . . " ' (Ex. 7:16).

You might be asking the obvious question, 'Why could they not worship him in Egypt? Why did they have to go to a special place?' They didn't, but they wanted to sacrifice and the Egyptians would not allow them to, they would have had to compromise in their worship in that land. Ironically once they did escape and get into the desert and had all the time in the world (forty years in fact!) to worship they were too busy grumbling and too busy building golden calves to worship a God who was not doing what they wanted and not doing it quickly enough!

At this point I think I would have given up – fortunately God did not! He had taken them out of Egypt to worship him in the desert. They seemed to need something tangible – as their building of the golden calf had shown – and the parting of seas, the appearance of manna, water gushing from rocks and pillars of cloud and fire was just not enough! Evidence of God was impressive but it was not permanent; it passed and people then, as now, had short memories. 'I need to be there in person,' I can imagine God saying, so for the first time ever, instead of just visiting, God would come to stay. God would live among them once they had built his 'house' – the tabernacle. If they played their part, he would fulfil his intention: 'The Lord said to Moses, "Tell the Israelites to bring me an offering. You are to receive the offering for me from each man whose heart prompts him to give. . . . Then have them make a sanctuary for me, and I will dwell among them' (Ex. 25:1, 8).

He was willing, if they were willing. The plans were very specific, but the people rallied round and in about eight and a half to nine months, the tabernacle had been completed. The ark was installed where God had told Moses, 'I will meet with you and give you all my commands for the Israelite people,' and all they were waiting for was for the architect himself to show up and take up residence in his new property! And show up he did! 'The cloud covered the Tent of the Meeting, and the glory of the Lord filled the tabernacle. Moses could not enter the Tent of the Meeting because the cloud had settled upon it, and the glory of the Lord filled the tabernacle' (Ex. 40:34–5). Just in case you didn't get it, the glory of the Lord filled the tabernacle! God had come and come to stay. From now on they would always be aware of his presence among them. 'In all the travels of the Israelites, whenever the cloud lifted from above the tabernacle, they would set out: but if the cloud did not lift, they did not set out – until the day it lifted. So the cloud of the Lord was over the tabernacle by day, and the fire was in the cloud by night, in the sight of all the house of Israel during all their travel' (Ex. 40:36–8).

God had never been so clear and so close; nothing could possibly go wrong. Or could it? From the moment the tabernacle was constructed and put in place, the seeds, which would one day leave the Samaritan woman and thousands like her out in the cold, had been sown. The Israelites lost the plot right at the start and were soon unable to see the wood for the trees, or their God for his tent. The tent was not a building. It was designed to be taken down and put back together on sand. It was not permanent; it was a means to an end. It was the place that showed the presence of God. It was the place Moses went to meet with God, but it was the meeting with God that was all important, not the place of the meeting. Moses knew that; he was not dependent on the tent, he was dependent on God.

When he pleaded with God for reassurance about the future, God simply said, 'My Presence will go with you and I will give you rest.' God had taken him up Mount Sinai and 'the Lord came down in the cloud and stood there with him and proclaimed his name, the Lord. And he passed in front of Moses, proclaiming, "The Lord, the Lord, the compassionate and gracious God, slow to anger, abounding in love and faithfulness, maintaining love to thousands, and forgiving wickedness, rebellion and sin" ' (Ex. 34: 5–7).

Perhaps it was because the Israelites always had to go through a priest that they themselves felt personally distant from God. Perhaps they got fed up with having to go through the same sacrificial rituals over and over again and never feeling clean. Whatever the cause, they soon found that the system and meeting place, which had been designed to draw them close to God, were in fact becoming a substitute for God. They went to the right place and said the right words, but their faces never shone because they never actually met with God. How many shiny faces do you see in your church on a Sunday? Again people had resorted to hiding from God, only this time it was more subtle, they actually hid in the things of God, the rituals, the ceremonies and the sacrifices and hoped he would not notice that they had left their hearts at home!

By the time the Israelites had arrived in the promised land and established themselves there, the tabernacle and the ark had got split up. Godly men, like Joshua, who had taken over as leader, when Moses died, were still building altars and making that connection with God in worship: 'Then Joshua built on Mount Ebal an altar to the Lord, the God of Israel, as Moses the servant of the Lord had commanded the Israelites. He built it according to what is written in the Book of the Law of Moses – an altar of uncut stones, on which no iron tool had been used. On it they offered to the Lord burnt offerings and sacrificed fellowship offerings' (Josh. 8:30–1).

There was still a genuineness in their worship. God had originally instructed them to build with raw stone as a picture of presenting their raw, in other words, real and unpolished, selves. They had been told that if they used a tool on it they would defile it. Why? Because once they made something to present, they would be proud of what they had made and be caught up in the look of the altar rather than the surrender of their unadorned selves. From the moment I first walked into a church I found myself asking, Why do people dress up for church on Sunday? I have heard the argument, 'You wouldn't visit the Queen of England in your old clothes would you? Then surely it is right to dress up for the king of the earth?' I think not. Just as God did not want them to be proud of their dressed altar then, he does not want us to be proud of our fancy clothes now. God wants you, your heart, he does not want a fashion parade. When a church implies that there is a right and acceptable way to dress, then the people who come into it are encouraged to think that everything is OK if they are wearing the right clothes, but not if they are not. You end up with the ridiculous and hilarious situation that was once photographed in Africa where early missionaries insisted that it was necessary for women to wear hats for church, so they did. They turned up naked, but apparently appropriately dressed because they had their hats on! In one sense it is irrelevant to God what we wear; it is when it is relevant to us that we have a problem. Being clothed in Jesus' righteousness is all that matters; it is and all God wants or needs to cover our sin, which is as filthy rags. Jesus rebuked those who gave the best seats to the best dressed and yet we are a society obsessed with the way we look and we are still doing it.

The Israelites found themselves living in a land where the inhabitants worshipped many false Gods. They were not atheists, as many are not today, but they did not believe in or worship the one true God. They felt the need for religion, so they created their own, and even those who should have known better, got drawn into their self-styled places of worship.

There is a very little, but very telling, incident in the book of Judges which shows how religion without God provides a place to go as a substitute for having a person to meet. We are introduced to a man named Micah, from the hill country of Ephraim:

> Now this man Micah had a shrine, and he made an ephod and some idols and installed one of his sons as his priest. In those days Israel had no king; everyone did as he saw fit.
>
> A young Levite from Bethlehem in Judah, who had been living with the clan of Judah, left that town in search of some other place to stay. On his way he came to Micah's house in the hill country of Ephraim.
>
> Micah asked him, 'Where are you from?'
>
> 'I'm a Levite from Bethlehem in Judah,' he said, 'And I'm looking for a place to stay.'
>
> Then Micah said to him, 'Live with me and be my father and my priest . . .' So the Levite agreed. . . . Then Micah installed the Levite and the young man became his priest and lived in his house. And Micah said, 'Now I know that the Lord will be good to me, since this Levite has become my priest' (Judg. 17:5–12).

What a shambles! And what a parallel I see with so much contemporary 'new age type religion' which replaces man being made in the image of God, with God actually being made in the image of man. In our desire to 'find ourselves' and call it a spiritual search, people are doing exactly what God told us not to do: making an idol, only the idol is 'self' and therefore totally justified in this age of enlightenment. Here we have Micah, a man who is hungry for God, building his own little place to worship and being aided and abetted by one of the true God's own people, a Levite, who had left the place he belonged, Judah, and been attracted by a religion which was man-made, on man's own terms, certainly not on God's terms. He allowed Micah to lean and depend on him 'like one of his own sons', not leading him to God, but actually getting in the way of God. The priesthood was set up to provide a link with God. Priests were chosen from the tribe of Levi, this man was a Levite but he was never supposed to play the role of father in

another person's life. No one but God is our father and there is
great danger in looking to a person to play that role in our
lives. Hundreds of years later Jesus would make this very
clear: 'And do not call anyone on earth "father", for you have
one Father and he is in heaven' (Mt. 23:9).

That would seem to be the problem! God is in heaven and
we can't see him, so we need to put something in his place,
either a building, or a person, like the local priest. We visit the
building and think we have visited God. We may well have
met with God because he promises that when we seek him, we
will find him, and that where two or three are gathered in his
name, he is there in the midst. But that has everything to do
with the attitude of our hearts and nothing to do with the
building itself. We go and talk to the priest, in some cases even
confess, and think we have had a dialogue with God. We may
have said our bit but he certainly has not said his and deep
down we know we are not forgiven because, 'Who can forgive
sins but God alone?' (Mk 2:7).

Before we leave the children of Israel in their new land we
need to see how things actually went from bad to worse in
their desire to substitute God with a person or a place. Let us
stay for a moment with the person. It wasn't long before the
people lost confidence in the judges, who had been put in place
to lead them, and began demanding a king. Poor Samuel was
the last of the judges and taking it very personally he turned to
God (so there were some people still on speaking terms with
him!). 'And the Lord told him: "Listen to all that the people are
saying to you; it is not you they have rejected, but they have
rejected me as their king. As they have done from the day I
brought them up out of Egypt until this day, forsaking me and
serving other gods, so they are doing to you' (1 Sam. 8:7–8).
Why did God not want them to have a king? Because he
wanted them to trust and obey him and to have a relationship
with him.

Despite the warnings Samuel gave the people about all the
dangers inherent in having a king, 'the people refused to listen

to Samuel. "No!" they said. "We want a king over us. Then we shall be like all the other nations, with a king to lead us and to go out before us and fight our battles" ' (1 Sam. 8:19). They had obviously forgotten God's wonderful promise to Moses all those years back when they were about to be swallowed up by Pharoah's army on the banks of the Red Sea: 'The Lord will fight for you; you need only be still' (Ex. 14:14). And he had – in spectacular ways! But they did not want to be still, they wanted to do something, to see someone they could look up to and obey like all the other nations. They had been called to be different. They had been called to put their trust in a God they could not see, but it was too hard. It would be so much easier to conform to the behaviour of those around them: it still is. God gave them what they wanted – a monarchy instead of a theocracy – and the closeness between God and his people was stretched almost to its limit. To keep his covenant on track, God's faithfulness had to match his people's unfaithfulness time and time again.

The first and one of the best kings God put in place was David, described as 'a man after God's own heart'. He was not perfect, but he wanted God's best in every situation and although he made some massive mistakes, his repentant heart always brought him back before the Lord, desperate to re-establish contact and be forgiven. It was his desire for God's best which led David to come up with the idea of a building, a house for God to dwell in now the tabernacle was on the high place at Gibeon and no longer up and running. David brought the ark from Abinadab's house and installed it in a little tent he had set up and then he had installed himself in a palace.

Lying there in luxury, he began to feel guilty about leaving God outside in the cold! 'After David was settled in his palace, he said to Nathan the prophet, "Here I am, living in a palace of cedar, while the ark of the covenant of the Lord is under a tent"' (1 Chron. 17:1). David was not allowed to build the house because he had shed too much blood. God reminded him that he was an ever-present God and could not be confined within four walls.

You are not the one to build me a house to dwell in. I have not
dwelt in a house from the day I brought Israel up out of Egypt to
this day. I have moved from one tent site to another, from one
dwelling-place to another. . . . Did I ever say 'Why have you not
built me a house of cedar? . . . I have been with you wherever you
have gone . . .' (1 Chron. 17:4b–6, 8).

David, you cannot put God in a box. You have got it all wrong:
you are not the one to build a house for me, ' . . . the Lord will
build a house for you.' The house God was concerned to build
would not be made of cedar or stone, it would be made of
people, it would be formed from the descendants of David, it
would be called the House of David and out of that house the
Lord Jesus himself would be born.

In the meantime God did allow David's son, Solomon, to
build the temple, so that the people would have somewhere to
come and sacrifice. When it was finished and the ark had been
put in place, the Lord filled the temple with his presence. The
temple of the Lord was filled with a cloud, and the priests
could not perform their service because of the cloud, for the
glory of the Lord filled the temple of God' (2 Chron. 5:13–4).
However, Solomon immediately realised that although God
was in the cloud, the cloud offered only a glimpse of God's
glory. God could not be confined to a box:

Then Solomon said, 'The Lord has said that he would
dwell in a dark cloud; I have built a magnificent temple
for you, a place for you to dwell for ever. (2 Chron. 6:1)

'But will God really dwell on earth with men? The heavens, even
the highest heavens, cannot contain you. How much less the
temple that I have built!' (2 Chron. 6:18).

God confirmed to Solomon that he had chosen this place as a
temple for sacrifices but it could and should never become a substitute for a relationship: prayer, not the place, was all important.

> If my people, who are called by my name, will humble themselves and pray and seek my face and turn from their wicked ways, then will I hear from heaven and will forgive their sin and will heal their land. . . . But if you turn away and forsake the decrees and commands I have given you and go off to serve other gods and worship them . . . I will reject this temple which I have consecrated for my Name. I will make it a byword and an object of ridicule among all peoples (2 Chron. 7:14, 19–20).

Don't just think you can turn up at the temple every so often and pay lip service to me when the rest of your life is lived in rebellion and unfaithfulness. One of the most common criticisms directed towards the church is that they are a bunch of hypocrites. They go to church on Sundays but you should see the way they live the rest of the week! Is that a resounding 'Amen!' I hear from heaven?! There is nothing God hates more than being honoured by peoples' lips when their hearts are far from him. You might be kidding yourself that in turning up at a certain place of worship you are doing your bit and God should be really impressed. Well he never has been, he never will be and neither will anyone else.

As the years went by, the children of Israel were taken into exile, the temple was destroyed and once they eventually returned, under the direction of Nehemiah, they had the task of rebuilding it all again. By now the ark had been lost and would only reappear when Indiana Jones went looking for it and Hollywood realised it would be in their best interests to let him lose it, almost as soon as he had found it! The possibility of follow-up films was endless!

Between the Old and the New Testament there are four hundred years of silence. God had continued to reach out and promise his people that if they returned to him, he would return to them. However, they were no longer on speaking terms; the distance between them had grown but it was not God who had moved (it never is!). Although we have seen how the building of God could be abused, it is fascinating to realise, that when God finally stepped out of heaven and came to live on earth, as Solomon has believed he never could, after such a long silence, the temple was still functioning and it was there that the faithful few could be found, still waiting for the Messiah and in the meantime serving as priests.

Jesus himself was protective of his 'Father's house', he turned out those who were exploiting the system to cover up their spiritual barrenness, he went there to learn and to teach and then one day he blew everything sky high by announcing, 'I tell you that one greater than the temple is here' (Mt. 12:6).

How was he greater than the temple? The temple had been the place to meet God: he was God! The temple had been the place to sacrifice: he was the sacrifice! The temple was no longer necessary and indeed in AD 70 it was destroyed for the last time. Jesus was the final sacrifice; no more blood needed to be shed. The temple had been the place where God came near, where he got up close and personal. Now God was here sitting on wells, talking to outcasts, he had come to dwell among men. So what happened when Jesus returned to heaven? Was the temple never mentioned again? Oh yes it was mentioned all right but now, amazingly, Paul says, 'Don't you know that you yourselves are God's temple and that God's Spirit lives in you' (1 Cor. 3:16). God has moved house! He no longer dwells in a tent, or puts his presence in a cloud in a building, he dwells in you by his spirit, when you have invited him to take up residence in your life. 'Do you not know that your body is a temple of the Holy Spirit, who is in you, who you have received from God?' (1 Cor. 6:19).

Of course we are jumping ahead here. Don't worry if you did not know this; the woman of Samaria did not know this and neither did anyone else who was hanging around with Jesus at the time. In fact the woman of Samaria was one of the first people Jesus chose to speak to about the spirit. But it is important to follow through with our question about the *where* of worship before we go on, in the next chapter, to look at what it means to worship in spirit and truth, the *how* and *who* of worship. Remember, we are trying to understand why people think God is to be found in a building. Why that old stone building on the corner of your street is called a church. We are back with the bricks again. First we saw them being piled on top of each other to form an altar, then stacked up to the sky to reach the heavens and lastly being carefully built into the temple. They were always to lead people to God, not to be a substitute for God. Now God dwells in people. The church is not a building, but it is made up of stones – living stones! 'As you come to him . . . you also, like living stones, are being built into a spiritual house to be a holy priesthood, offering spiritual sacrifices acceptable to God through Jesus Christ' (1 Pet. 2:5). The house is there, the priesthood is there, the sacrifices are there, but they are all invisible to the human eye, they are all in Christ. 'In him the whole building is joined together and rises to become a holy temple in the Lord. And in him you too are being built together to become a dwelling in which God lives by his Spirit' (Eph. 2:21–2).

The Samaritan woman had got it all wrong when she laid so much emphasis on the place of worship, but then, so have many who don't know Christ, along with many who do! I so often go into the church building on a Sunday and hear people pray, 'As we come into your presence Lord . . . ' We don't come into his presence in the building, if we have been born again of his Spirit we live in his presence and his presence lives in us. Do those who pray that prayer think we go out of his presence as we leave the church building? Christians themselves make up the body of Christ – the church. It was a very sad day when the first ornate building was put up, the temple mentality was reestablished and many well-meaning people began attending a place with no understanding that it all pointed to a person, who was longing to have relationship with them, but whom they lost somewhere in the stained-glass windows.

'God is spirit and his worshippers must worship in spirit and in truth' (Jn. 4:24). As we have seen this had never happened; so why was Jesus telling her it was what she must do? How would a many times divorced Samaritan woman be able to succeed where generations of Israelites had failed? Was it possible? *Yes!* How can I make those little letters enormous enough on the page to let you catch their huge affirmation? *Yes.* Because God was here, in Jesus he was up closer and more personal than he had ever been. So close that by his spirit he would actually invade the heart and live there. So personal that the encounter would be painful. So possible because the God who had said no one could ever see his face and live had now stepped out of eternity and out of the temple to look this woman straight in the eyes and declare, 'I who speak to you am he.'

Chapter 8

Our Father

'Our fathers worshipped on this mountain . . .'

God had come looking for individuals since Adam and Eve had hidden among the trees. People had continued hiding and up until this point the Samaritan woman herself was doing a pretty good job of hiding too, sheltering behind the beliefs of her forefathers. But Jesus is God, he was still seeking, and he would not be deterred. He picks up what she is saying about fathers, catching her idea and developing it. So often, we slam people down when we are talking to them about God, batting their ideas away and giving them an awful sense of rejection. He does not. He hears her words and runs with them, developing the whole idea of father to Father. He speaks to her about, 'the kind of worshippers the Father seeks', showing her that God is still actually in the business of seeking and that if she would only step out of the shadows she would realise she had been found. She is like the little boy playing hide and seek with his face in a cushion on the settee and his bottom sticking up in the air for all the world to see, shouting, 'You can't see me!' Just because we can't see God, even when he is right under our noses, as he was in this case, does not mean he can't see us! God had always been able to see her and now he has come in person to make her an offer which she will soon realise she can't refuse: 'God is spirit, and his worshippers must worship in spirit and truth' (Jn. 4:24).

Up to this point she had been a vague believer. What would it take to transform her into a worshipper: one who gives God his place of worth in her life? It would take three things:

- Knowing him as her Father
- Receiving the Spirit
- Responding in truth.

These would have been mind-blowing concepts for this woman or any woman, just like me, who had grown up with some vague religious system passed down to them by previous generations, all about being from the right people, and being found in the right place to reach God and not about allowing him to find me and have a personal relationship with me.

Knowing him as Father

Up until this point Jesus has spoken about God, now he introduces one of his intimate names: Father. This may be very familiar to those who have recited 'Our Father, who art in heaven' in dreary unison, along with hundreds of other primary school children, but it certainly was not a familiar concept to the Samaritan woman. To understand why it would take a big shift in her thinking to see God as her father, we need to go back to the Old Testament and find out who, if anyone, called him that. Hopefully, this may help us understand why we find it difficult or easy for this woman, and for us, to see God as our Father.

I have heard many people say that we are *all* God's children. This may be reassuring but it is simply not true. In the Old Testament God is never referred to as the Father of mankind, but he is frequently referred to as the Father of a chosen nation. He chose the children of Israel to be his children. He set up the possibility of having a close, personal relationship with people on earth, yet, as we have just seen, in this relationship he faced constant rejection. Certain individuals saw him in this role and rebuked those who gave him the cold shoulder. Listen to Moses,

> I will proclaim the name of the Lord.
>> Oh, praise the greatness of our God!
> He is the Rock, his works are perfect,
>> and all his ways are just.
> A faithful God who does no wrong,
>> upright and just is he.
> They have acted corruptly toward him;
>> to their shame they are no longer his children,
>> but a warped and crooked generation.
> Is this the way you repay the Lord,
>> O foolish and unwise people?
> Is he not your Father, your Creator,
>> who made you and formed you? (Deut. 32:3–6).

God had not just made the people of Israel, he had made them his sons (which includes daughters!) and there are many pictures of how he lovingly cared for them. 'The Lord your God carried you, as a father carries his son, all the way you went until you reached this place' (Deut. 1:31). He put his child, the nation of Israel, in difficult situations, but was always there to protect and enable:

> In a desert land he found him,
>> in a barren and howling waste.
> He shielded him and cared for him;
>> he guarded him as the apple of his eye,
> like an eagle that stirs up its nest,
>> and hovers over its young,
> that spreads its wings to catch them
>> and carries them on its pinions.
> The Lord alone led him;
>> no foreign god was with him (Deut. 32:10–12).

The parent bird has to stir up the nest to encourage its young to leave it and to fly. When the little one sets off, with those first few tentative test flights, the parent does an amazing thing: it hovers close by and swoops to catch the fledgling on its back as soon as it needs help, carrying it to a safe place. This is exactly what God had done as he coaxed his children out of Egypt.

Human fathers always have limits. God knew that and patiently showed his people that they could transfer their trust from their earthly fathers to him. 'When your days are over and you go to be with your fathers, I will raise up your offspring to succeed you, one of your own sons, and I will establish his kingdom. . . . I will be his father, and he will be my son. . . . I will never take my love away from him . . . his throne will be established for ever' (1 Chron. 17:11–14). God was speaking to David about the line that would come through him which would be everlasting. All human fathers die: our heavenly father does not. As we saw in the previous chapter, God's children refused to trust him. He could have rejected them, but his fatherly love, so beautifully expressed in Hosea, would not give up:

> When Israel was a child, I loved him,
>   and out of Egypt I called my son.
> But the more I called Israel,
>   the further they went from me. . . .
> It was I who taught Ephraim to walk,
>   taking them by the arms;
> but they did not realise
>   it was I who healed them.
> I led them with cords of human kindness,
>   with ties of love;
> I lifted the yoke from their neck
>   and bent down to feed them (Hos. 11:1–4).

What an amazingly tender image this is of God intimately involved in child-rearing! He called to his child, he reached out and touched his child, supporting his toddler under his arms as he took his first few teetering steps, and he bent down to spoon feed his infant. It was a wonderful privilege to be the chosen children of God, but this wilful nation was typical of the rest of us; they did not appreciate all he had done for them and how much he loved them. They refused to love him. And still feeling the need to love and be loved, as we all do, they created absurd idols as substitutes: They say to the wood, 'You are my father,' and to the stone, 'You gave me birth' (Jer. 2:27). What an insult to God! The simple words 'Abba, Father', were not on their lips and the longer he waited the more hard-hearted they became. God has to admit,

> I myself said,
> 'How gladly would I treat you like sons
>   and give you a desirable land,
> the most beautiful inheritance of any nation.'
> I thought you would call me 'Father'
>   and not turn away from following me.
> But like a woman unfaithful to her husband,
>   so you have been unfaithful to me,
>   O house of Israel,'
> declares the Lord (Jer. 3:19–20).

The children of Israel only turned to God when they needed help. Like many of us in today's world they saw him a bit like a fire extinguisher, standing by, waiting to be used when the heat was on. They did not want a relationship with him as a father. Like my friend, who promised God she would serve him if he would only give her the man she wanted to marry, but did not keep her promises when the emergency was over. She used him and moved on to do her own thing, not wanting to submit to his authority or surrender to his love. 'Have we not all one Father? Did not one God create us?' (Mal. 2:10). In other words, 'We're OK. We're all children of God.' But they were not OK. They neither knew God nor were they able to lead people into a relationship with him. God would have to come to earth in human form to reach humanity. He would have to send his son so that we could become his sons and daughters. He had loved his chosen people but they had rejected him. His love would now be released on the world and each person would have the choice as to whether or not they would accept that love and choose him as their father.

I find that remarkably humbling. Once, humans came and offered sacrifices in worship to a holy God. It was his choice whether or not our sacrifices were acceptable. Now we have the choice. God sent his son as the sacrifice for the sins of the world. He offers himself to each one of us and we choose whether or not we will accept his sacrifice on our behalf. He gives; he cannot force us to receive. This choice is made in a moment in time and yet this choice has eternal consequences: 'God so loved the world that he gave his one and only Son, that whoever believes in him shall not perish but have eternal life' (Jn. 3:16).

The woman of Samaria was clinging on for all she was worth to the religion of her 'fathers', trusting what they had told her about worship but probably never allowing it to make any real difference to her life. She was perishing. If pushed, she would no doubt have said she believed God was her father through Jacob. Whether he was or wasn't, it no longer mattered. What mattered was the choice she was being forced to make about the person sitting talking to her, delaying her from filling her pot with water, in order to hold out the water of life to her. Was he telling the truth? Could she trust him?

These are the two questions I, and in fact all of us, have to face if we are going to make the transition from being a creation of God to being a child of God. Before we consider why that might be harder for some than others, let us look at how it is possible now for anyone, anywhere, to become a child of God, rather than just that special line of people who were connected to the house of Israel.

Jesus' arrival on earth heralded the beginning of a new era. No longer was access to the family of God reserved for the chosen few, it was now open to everyone. No longer would the priests be the only ones who could get close to God in the holy of holies. The moment Jesus died on the cross, the huge curtain in the temple, which kept ordinary people distant from and outside that special meeting place, was ripped from top to bottom. The great high priest, Jesus, had blazed a trail into heaven and into the presence of God and the route was open to us all. Being a child of God was no longer a question of birthright, it was now a question of belief.

The whole of John's gospel, which includes the story of the Samaritan woman, was written, 'that you may believe that Jesus Christ is the Son of God, and that by believing you may have life in his name' (Jn. 20:31). Right from the start, John explains to the reader what that life is and how it is now available to all people to receive so that they can actually become children of God. The Jews had become complacent. The majority had no relationship with God, they simply had a set of rules which had hardened their hearts. The harder they found it to obey, the harder they became on those 'beneath' them, and the more judgemental they became on those who didn't. Ironically, in the name of religion they condemned Jesus, God himself, because he did not fit inside their little box. He broke the rules, and the more religious you become, the more the rules matter. He touched people you shouldn't touch. He ate on days you should fast. He partied with sinful people and he made claims about himself, that seemed blasphemous. In a self-righteous effort to defend the name of God, they actually rejected God. 'He was in the world, and though the world was made through him, the world did not recognise him. He came to that which was his own, but his own did not receive him (Jn. 1: 10–11).

And yet, as John continues, to all who received him, to those who believed in his name, he gave the right to become children of God – children born not of natural descent, not of human decision or of a husband's will, but born of God.' (Jn. 1:12a–13). It's that simple: recognise him, believe in him and receive him.

Those three steps will transform you from being a creature, made by a creator, to being a child, indwelt by the Spirit and loved by the Father. They transport you from being simply a dweller in time to being a dweller in space: timeless eternity. Children of God live for ever because the life you receive when you believe is the very life of God himself. He does not hand out a package from heaven, this is not a gift *from* God as such: he comes himself from heaven, first as Jesus and then as the Holy Spirit; this is the gift *of* God. To put this into the Samaritan woman's frame of reference, Jesus had spoken of water rather than the spirit, but he was explaining the same truth. ' If you knew the gift *of* God and who it is that asks you for a drink, you would have asked him and he would have given you living water. . . . whoever drinks the water I give him will never thirst. Indeed, the water I give him will become in him a spring of water welling up to eternal life' (Jn. 4:10, 14).

The first (and only!) time we were born, we did not choose who our father would be or whether or not we would even be born at all. Now Jesus is saying you have the chance to start again; only this time you do have a choice and having made the choice all you have to do is ask. The first time you were born of water, the second time will be of the Spirit, just as Jesus told Nicodemus: 'I tell you the truth, no one can enter the kingdom of God unless he is born of water and the Spirit. Flesh gives birth to flesh, but the Spirit gives birth to spirit' (Jn. 3:5). We have made it so complicated; God made it so simple. 'This is the testimony: God has given us eternal life, and this life is in his Son. He who has the Son has life; he who does not have the Son of God does not have life' (1 Jn. 5:11–12). Where you were born is no longer relevant. How you were born, whether you were 'planned' or not, is not important. Who your forefathers were does not carry any weight when it comes to receiving eternal life. The only thing that matters is whether, when you recognise Jesus, you believe in him and receive him and this is where for many, it becomes complicated. You might well say the choice is very clear and oh so obvious, but for me it is so difficult. I find it hard to jump into the arms of my heavenly father and surrender to becoming his child, because I did that to my earthly father and he let me fall, he let me down and now I do not know if I can ever really trust again.

If you had the most wonderful father, you may find it difficult to understand why some people find it hard to even say the name 'father' without being overwhelmed with negative feelings, and you may be tempted to skip this next section. Let me encourage you to read on because if you don't struggle over this issue, you could well be friends with, or be married to someone who does and your understanding could actually make all the difference.

A child's relationship with their father is one of the key relationships in that child's life. It is a very necessary relationship and to be deprived of it can have far-reaching effects. Whereas most of us know who our mothers are, some people have no idea who their father is, and this can leave a child feeling rejected and very alone. I have seen those who know they came out of a sperm bank interviewed on television and for some, the desire to find the donor, their father, can become an all-consuming passion. It is not just knowing, but being known, which is so important. One girl, conceived from a sperm bank, prepared a photo album and story of her life to present to the father she had never known, but had managed to track down. After two attempts to see him and pluck up the courage to tell him who she was, she turned away at the last minute, clutching the secrets of who she was close to her heart when she so obviously wished she could put them into her father's heart. I hope one day the transfer may happen and her sense of belonging may be restored. Although adopted children are usually extremely grateful for the couple who have brought them up, they are often left with questions about their real identity which can take them on a lifelong search. Years ago the adoptive parents were able to conceal the identity of the real parents, this is no longer the case because the powers that be have realised it is not simply a fundamental right to know who your parents are, it is a fundamental need.

'God sets the lonely in families' (Prov. 68:6), presumably so that they will no longer be lonely. God made families to give each person a sense of security and belonging. It is very freeing to know your little picture is part of a big picture; it started long before you were ever around and will continue long after you have gone. One of my daughters has her Granny's forehead! The other has her Grandpa's smile, and people are always saying to my son, 'You are so like your dad.' My children have a place in this world; they have talents and mannerisms that they have inherited. If they are lucky enough to have their own children, they will no doubt see that the pattern goes on.

I believe that our awareness of our place in our family whispers to us of eternity. We need to belong to something that stretches beyond time and there is a mystery in the seed of likeness and life as it reappears in countless generations. I had a friend who felt this was eternal life. He was dying but he believed that in some way he would go on in his children. That is not eternal life, but it does hint at the possibility of ongoing life which can be found in Christ. Whereas we can pass biological family traits from one generation to the next, we cannot give his Spirit to our children. Because God is my Father he is not my children's grandfather. He is no one's grandfather! They, like me, have the wonderful privilege of asking him if they can be his child only to discover he is more than willing to be their father.

It always amazes me that however awful an earthly father can be to his child, the child longs to give the father the benefit of the doubt and will always give him just one more chance. In his wonderful book, *Angela's Ashes*, Frank McCourt tells the story of a family caught in the most desperate poverty trap in Ireland in the early twentieth century. While the mother of the family picks coal off the street to keep her children warm and continually compromises her sense of dignity by lining up for handouts, the father behaves in the most irresponsible, immature and erratic manner. He drinks away any little money he earns, forces the children to get out of bed in the middle of the night to sing Republican songs and constantly lets the family down.

Nevertheless, Frank longs to believe in and be known by his father. He hungers for time alone with him. They go for walks in the countryside; they dream together; and Frank hangs on to his father's promises no matter haw many times he breaks them. This is not unusual. I now believe that the longing to be known intimately by our parents (well disguised during the touchy 'leave-me-alone' teenage years) is a response to a very deep awareness that we are indeed known by someone, somewhere: God. 'Before I formed you in the womb, I knew you' (Jer. 1:5). We sense he is out there somewhere and yet until we have found him, we long to be known and look to those we are closest to, to fulfil that longing.

In messy divorces children find themselves waiting to be picked up by absent fathers at the weekend, refusing to admit that as time goes by their father has moved on and, most hurtful of all, has often put someone else, often a pretty little woman and then a cute little baby, in their place. This may sound cynical but I have witnessed it countless times among my friends and seen the anguish and sense of abandonment it inevitably causes. He is now putting his time into knowing someone else's children, while his own children still crave that special place in his heart. Why do children cling so tenaciously to this image of a trustworthy, loving father, when in truth they have never and will never know one. I can only conclude it is because God has put eternity in the heart of each human being. Not a faceless, impersonal eternity, but an eternity where someone is in control and that someone is loyal and faithful and can be relied upon. To me a child's longing to believe in the perfect father figure, against all the odds, is evidence that he exists; and he does, though not on earth, but in heaven!

Along with all those who are sad that they have never known their fathers, there are many who, if they could be totally honest, would say they wish that they had never known their fathers! It is very popular in this day and age to hold our fathers responsible for all our personal struggles. We have this simple equation embedded in our psyche: they failed us as children and that is why we are failing as adults. Although I have great sympathy with the pain and struggles that lead to this equation, I realise that it is too simplistic. There are hundreds of books which explore the damage done by hundreds of fathers and they have been a huge help to many hurting people, but this path has been well trodden and I feel challenged to introduce a different perspective.

We have a picture of an ideal father, which we impose on our real father, and most can do nothing but fail. The modern father is supposed to spend regular time with his children. Surveys have been done to prove that on average he spends 27 seconds a day, one-on-one with each of his children and is therefore a failure. He is supposed to be sensitive, willing to express his emotions and listen to those of his children. He is supposed to be many things, which his wife is probably more aware of than he is, and his children would certainly not be aware of unless some well meaning counsellor pointed them out as the reason a particular child may be failing, may be aggressive, etc. I am not belittling the effect the father can have in the child's life, but I am aware that our expectations may be becoming totally unrealistic and with them we will only produce a whole generation of failing fathers.

Not only do we hold these standards up against contemporary fathers, we also go marching back in time and thrust them in the faces of all those fathers who came out of the war years. In my desire to understand my father, I try and understand why my father was who he was, in the context of his home environment and his generation. Many men of his era were brought up to believe they were the 'head of the home'. Their own parents had come through the Victorian reign, where what the man said went (unless of course they happened to be married to Queen Victoria!). They often worked hard at jobs, which in a different life they would not have chosen. Coming straight out of the forces, they had to do something and do it fast. They had a loyalty to the cause of rebuilding their country which most of us know little about. They had been forced to keep their emotions bottled up as they watched their fellow soldiers, sailors and airmen being blasted to pieces. They had grown used to living in a structured, regimented lifestyle, which left little room for freedom of expression. They had to deny themselves for the greater cause as they said goodbye to their sweethearts, who they knew they may not see for years, if ever. They had never heard of focusing on the family and giving your children 'quality time'! They worked long, hard hours to feed the family and that was their point of focus. They had no parenting manual. Parenting was just something they did, there was nothing to learn about it. These were our parents. Many of them failed when held up against today's expectations, but so do many parents of our generation, and we have all the guidance, relevant literature and parenting seminars we could ever want.

Whatever your experience of your father may have been, each of us has a choice to make. You did not have a choice about who he would be, you did not have a choice about the way he would treat you, but you do have a choice about what effect you will allow your upbringing to have on you now. You are not responsible for what has happened, but you are responsible for how you deal with what has happened and here lies the problem. So many see themselves as victims and live out lives that do not deal with the pain, but simply strive to anaesthetise it. They are prisoners of the past as we saw in Chapter 4.

What kind of father did the Samaritan woman have? We are not told. It would be all too easy to summise that he could not have been a good one or she would not have been so promiscuous. When they are growing up girls need appropriate affection from their fathers, and if they don't receive that affection then later in life their craving for affirmation and intimacy can lead to promiscuity. She is not responsible for the cause of her behaviour, but she is responsible for her behaviour, as we all are. Understanding why we do what we do and continually excusing what we do are very different. Children who have had wonderful fathers may well become wonderful fathers, they may also choose to rebel and cause their own children real pain. I know boys who have grown up with no father, yet they have become good fathers. God himself, as we have seen, was a loyal and loving parent. Were his children grateful? Did they become good fathers? No they did not – far from it! There are many stories of weak parenting in the Bible; in fact apart from God himself, there is no one (except Boaz possibly) a father would want to model himself on. Abraham, Isaac, Jacob, David, Saul, Solomon and many others all displayed what we would call inadequate fathers who created dysfunctional families.

The message that seems to come through loud and clear is that when we put the bar so high that we almost demand perfection, it becomes impossible for a parent to succeed. Failing is part of being human and is experienced by both child and parent alike. There is only one father who will never fail and that is our heavenly Father. If the failure of our earthly father prevents us putting our trust in our heavenly Father, then we have missed the point. We are all sinners in need of forgiveness. When I see my parents as a people in need, sinners just like me, I can stand alongside them and realize, with compassion and love, that we all need the Saviour. They have provided me with much I am very thankful for, but like me, they have made mistakes. I thank God for maturity and distance, which have allowed times of openness, honesty and restoration. The more I know my heavenly parent, the more I value my relationships with my earthly parents and marvel at the way they continue to evolve and deepen.

We can hide behind hurt from our parents to such an extent that it becomes our whole identity. Unable to think outside that hurt, we refuse to acknowledge that a heavenly Father may succeed where an earthly parent has failed, and we do not give him a chance. Human disappointment can be a stepping stone to God or a stumbling block which leaves us tripping over, face down, unwilling to look up and see him patiently waiting.

Receiving the Spirit

'It is impossible,' you might want to scream. 'I have been abused, confused, misused . . . I will never be able to see God as a father and surrender in trust as a child. I will never again say the word, "Daddy." I just can't. I am afraid. My heart is closed, my lips are sealed and I will never be free to worship him. I will never . . .' Stop! I have wonderful news for you. You, in your own strength, battling with your own conflict, may not be free to worship, may resist giving God his rightful place in your life, but by Jesus' Spirit you can do it. Look carefully at these amazing words from Paul:

> So also, when we were children, we were in slavery under the basic principles of the world. But when the time had fully come, God sent his Son, born of a woman, born under law, to redeem those under law, that we might receive the full rights of sons. Because you are sons, God sent the Spirit of his Son into our hearts, the Spirit who calls out, 'Abba, Father.' So you are no longer a slave, but a son; and since you are a son, God has made you also an heir' (Gal. 4:3–7).

Once you are born again, you are indwelt by his Spirit. You are his child, free to see him as your father. You are no longer a slave to the relationship you had with your earthly father. His Spirit will free your tongue to cry out, 'Daddy!'

'The true worshippers will worship the Father in spirit and truth.' 'It's impossible for you,' Jesus is saying, 'but it is possible for me. The choice as to whether you let me do that, whether you drink the water I am offering, is yours, and the time has now come for you to make that choice.' God cannot be worshipped in your own strength. This is not a religion that asks you to adhere to a set of rules, but a relationship which calls for a total response from your inner being. Whatever hurts and reservations lay buried deep within you, naturally preventing you from worshipping God as your Father, they can be overcome when Jesus by his Spirit takes up residence in your inner being.

One of the first verses in the Bible I ever learnt was 2 Timothy 1:7: 'For God did not give us a spirit of fear, but of power and of love and of a sound mind' (AV). You don't need to be afraid. Jesus lives in you and when you can't come to the Father, he can take you to him because God is his Father too and together you can cry, 'Abba!' With thousands upon thousands we can unite and pray 'Our Father . . . ' – words the Jews would never have used because of their familiarity.

He united himself with his disciples when they asked him to teach them to pray and he still does. Even when we can't put it into words, he can: 'The Spirit helps us in our weakness. We do not know what we ought to pray, but the Spirit himself intercedes for us with groans that words cannot express. And he who searches our hearts knows the mind of the Spirit, because the Spirit intercedes for the saints in accordance with God's will' (Rom. 8:26–7).

'I can't call him father; I can't worship in Spirit.' Saying 'I can't' is very different from saying 'I won't.' When you say 'I can't', it suggests that really you want to but feel unable. A friend of mine has this life-releasing little saying, 'I can't and you never said I could. You can and you always said you would.' When you say 'I won't', then you are saying you are not willing. Jesus cannot give anything to you if you will not reach out your hand and take what he is offering – the gift of God. Maybe there is something in your hand that needs to be put down before it is empty enough to receive anything else: hurt from your childhood; resentment from you parent's divorce; your determination to solve your own problems. It is your choice.

We know, if we jump to the end of the story and witness the woman leaving her water pot and therefore her own resources behind, that she made her choice. But before we move on to see her being able to walk away from her past and tell the truth in a way she probably never had before, I want to explore what Jesus meant when he talked about worshipping in truth. Apart from the struggle she, and many others, faced and continue to face, over calling God her Father, did she also have a problem with facing the truth and therefore being able to worship in truth? It's a key question, which calls for another chapter!

Chapter 9

Facing the Truth

'. . . true worshippers will worship the Father in
spirit and truth . . .'

Before we even consider the idea of worshipping in truth we need to explore whether or not we live our lives in truth. Most of us play games in conversations, maneuvering around the truth rather than revealing the truth. The conversation Jesus has with the woman at the well is a fascinating study in how one person can enable another person to be honest with themselves and eventually with the person they are talking to. You cannot force the truth out of a person, they have to be willing to give it to you. I have always said to my own children and students, as they told me a story which seemed a little suspect, 'Look me in the eyes and tell me that again.' I remember a situation years ago when I suspected a girl of stealing and then lying to cover up what she had done. As I questioned her about her whereabouts at certain times and asked her to show me what she had in her pockets, she answered in monosyllables and kept her eyes fixed on the ground and her hands stuck in her pockets. I could not make her tell me the truth and to this day I do not know whether or not she stole the money, but I do know she found it hard to look me in the face.

It has been said that the eyes are the windows of the soul. We have a God-given conscience and when we lie, we violate that conscience and it shows in our eyes. I think it is remarkable

that we can 'see into' someone's thoughts and feelings simply
by looking into their eyes. I certainly couldn't do that with our
guinea pigs! The divine spark seen in the eyes is part of the
uniqueness of being human. Our eyes register love, hate, fear,
lying, amusement, anger and many other emotions that we
may believe we can leave buried in our hearts and no one will
ever know they are there. I wonder if the woman of Samaria
cast her eyes down as she was drawn deeper and deeper into
truth by this amazing man. In some ways she was quite feisty
and bold as she challenged and questioned him and I can
imagine she did look at him, but with shutters on her eyes.

I used to work with Witness Support in the high court near
where I lived in England. I helped prepare prosecution
witnesses to go and stand in the witness box and give a clear
and honest testimony. They needed practical and emotional
support and when they first arrived at court I would take them
and show them the courtroom and give them the opportunity
to stand in the box that they would soon have to climb into,
which was very high and rather intimidating. I would always
show them the card they would have to read to promise they
would tell the truth before they gave their testimony. They
could swear 'by Almighty God that the evidence they would
give would be the truth, the whole truth and nothing but the
truth', or they could leave God out of it and just promise to tell
the truth.

It always amazed me that the whole court system is built on
the belief that people will actually tell the truth. If there was
ever any evidence that there is an absolute God, a truth outside
of ourselves, then that is it! We may deny there is a God but we
accept that each person has a conscience and will listen to that
conscience and justice will be done. Without knowing it, we are
affirming what God explained in his Word, that 'when
Gentiles, who do not have the law, do by nature things
required by the law, they are a law for themselves, even though
they do not have the law, since they show that the requirements
of the law are written on their hearts, their consciences also

bearing witness, and their thoughts now accusing, now defending them' (Rom. 2:14–15). In the final analysis, when all the evidence has been given, no one in a court really knows the truth except God and the defendant, the one being accused of the crime, and no one can force it out of him. 'The Lord does not look at the things man looks at. Man looks at the outward appearance, but the Lord looks at the heart' (1 Sam. 16:7b). The jury tries to arrive at the truth by piecing together what they hear and see of the witnesses, but they can easily come to the wrong conclusion and a guilty man can go free and an innocent man be imprisoned. They cannot see into the heart, where the truth lies buried.

The problem, for most of us, is that we don't know the truth about ourselves, so even when we do try and verbalise accurately what we think and feel, we are not honest. We twist things, leave things out, emphasise certain things and usually paint ourselves in a good light. 'The heart is deceitful above all things and beyond cure' (Jer. 17:9). On the whole, self-interest dictates our thinking and although it may not be deliberate, much of what we say is manipulative. We want the listener to come round to our way of thinking. We want them to do what we want and we use many subtle means to cajole and influence. What comes out of our mouths started in our hearts. As Jesus told the Pharisees, 'Out of the overflow of the heart the mouth speaks' (Mt. 12:34).

When we get into conversation with people we tell them only what we want them to know. Only the careful listener will probe beyond the words presented, to access what lies beneath. We often talk casually about things that have nothing to do with what is really going on deep within us, hoping to deflect those who wander too close to the truth. It takes time and trust to draw out the real person behind the face and within the words. The Beatles created a character, in one of their songs, called Eleanor Rigby. What a sad, unforgettable image they created as they described how she put on a mask that she kept in a jar by the door. How many masks do you keep in your jar?

Do you have special ones for special occasions: the 'happy, isn't-life-fun?' mask, the 'I-am-strong-nothing-can-hurt-me' mask, the 'I-am-so-spiritual, gentle smile mask', usually slipped on as you rush out of the door to church! Only those looking with God's eyes see behind the mask.

Obviously we have different levels of conversation with those we meet depending on the circumstances. Most words we exchange fit into one of these levels:

1. Cliches – 'Nice day today isn't it?'
2. Facts – 'I am going to visit my friend.'
3. Opinions – 'I think the roads are going to be busy.'
4. Feelings – 'I am nervous about seeing my friend.'
5. Transparent honesty – 'We haven't seen each other for six months because last time we were together, we argued and I am not sure if she will even open the door to me.'

If we are looking with God's eyes and listening behind the words presented then I believe we can move through these levels even with a perfect stranger who we happen to be standing next to as we both wait for a bus! The right questions, asked in the right way can unlock a person's heart. It has been said, 'When I understand what you are thinking I am in the passageway of your life. When I understand what you are feeling I am in the living room of your life.' Many people are lonely and have never had anyone in their actual living room for years, so to let them into that private space in their hearts can be really threatening. You can only get as close to someone as their honesty will allow. I love the opportunity of meeting strangers and under God's prompting, making my way through the levels of communication until I find myself sitting with them having a cup of tea and wishing the plane journey or time in the waiting room could last a bit longer. There is no greater privilege than to have someone share their secrets with you, allowing you access to the place that only God can see.

It is Larry Crabb who says,

We must not yield to the urge to retreat into the silence of safe, superficial chatter. We must keep talking. And our words must matter. They must reveal what is most shamefully true about us. The richest conversations always tell a story. Both the storyteller and the listener need to hear the doubting soul struggling to find identity. They need to look eagerly for the movement of God that frees people to give, to be and to worship. (*Isn't this exactly what Jesus is doing as he talks to and listens to the woman at the well?*) . . . Encourage others to tell their stories to you. Ask questions that require people to think about their experience, to visualize scenes in their lives that provoke deep feelings. 'What was it like for you to walk into that hospital room?' . . . Good conversations are often disturbing. They deal with the edge in someone's voice that puts others on guard . . . Good conversations uncover the terror and rage that often lie hidden beneath a veneer of comfortable relationship.[9]

As Jesus sat on the well, in the heat of the day, he very gently led the woman before him to face the truth about herself, so that he could reveal the truth about himself. She is obviously very preoccupied with the practicalities of drawing water, but it is all a cover for the hurting relationships and the confused religion which churned about within her and which no doubt caused too much pain to face head on. The truth about her lies buried under years of coping with prejudice and isolation. Facing that truth takes on a whole new meaning when 'I am the truth' is literally staring her in the face! If she can just surface from under her burdens for a moment and look into that face – and what a face it must have been! – she will actually see truth for the first time and not be threatened by it. His eyes must have penetrated deep beneath the surface and although she does not realise it at first, the revelation of the truth about who she is will be the most freeing thing she has ever experienced and the one thing she wants to tell everyone. In a few moments she will find herself exhorting her neighbours to 'Come see a man who told me everything I ever did!' The truth is not a set of beliefs to argue over with the Jews, or something that was irrevocably lost long ago in all her broken relationships, the truth is a person called Jesus, and 'the truth will set you free'.

The idea of looking into the face of God and not just being freed, but actually living to tell the tale and to worship him in truth was a revolutionary concept. As the woman listened to Jesus and her yearning for the Messiah began to find expression, Jesus said, 'I who speak to you am he' (Jn. 4:26). Apparently the word 'he' is not part of the original text and what Jesus was really saying was, 'I AM is speaking to you.' 'I AM' was God's name from the Old Testament, spoken as 'Jehovah', and by using it Jesus was letting her know that God himself was sitting beside her: he had come and she was literally facing the Truth.

God had always been the truth and had always spoken the truth, and he had always longed for his people to respond to him in truth.

> I have not spoken in secret,
>   from somewhere in a land of darkness;
> I have not said to Jacob's descendents,
>   'Seek me in vain.'
> I, the Lord, speak the truth;
>   I declare what is right (Is. 45:19).

It was very convenient for the Jews to think of God as distant and impersonal. As we saw earlier, they went through the motions of their ritualistic religion, hoping he was too far away to notice there was no truth or reality left in their worship. But God was not fooled. 'Truth has perished,' Jeremiah tells us. 'It has stumbled in the streets and is nowhere to be found,' Isaiah laments. Sooner or later whatever is going on in the heart finds its way out of the mouth. Those who don't speak the truth don't just say nothing; they speak lies:

> 'Friend deceives friend,
>   and no one speaks the truth.
> They have taught their tongues to lie:
>   they weary themselves with sinning.
> You live in the midst of deception:
>   in their deceit they refuse
> to acknowledge me,'
> declares the Lord (Jer. 9:5–6).

Those who don't worship the true God don't just worship nothing, they worship lies and idols. As Paul explains, they, 'suppress the truth by their wickedness . . . They exchanged the truth of God for a lie, and worshipped and served created things rather than the Creator' (Rom. 1:18, 25). Religion detached from God himself becomes dishonest and hypocritical. If you don't have a relationship with God, then turning up for worship is just hard work, which you end up doing with no heart or not doing at all. Going to church when you don't know God is a chore, and now the days of doing it to appear respectable in front of the local community are over, most who are 'true to themselves' don't bother. Once you have decided there is no God, then there is no one outside of yourself to obey and what may at first have felt like disobedience initially feels like freedom and you can't get enough of it. But God is still there and he is still true and because he has planted a conscience within each of us we will never be happy living in denial of the truth.

We may have lost sight of the truth, as the chosen people did, but we still yearn for it and God is only too eager to reintroduce us to truth himself, to Jesus, 'the glory of the One and Only, who came from the Father, full of grace and truth' (Jn. 1:14). Lying had become a way of life for the majority of God's people, so it is hardly surprising that after four hundred years of silence Jesus bursts on the scene and prefaces nearly everything he says with, 'I tell you the truth . . . ' What a relief! It's about time somebody did. Jesus explained to a very confused Pilate that he had come into the world 'to testify to the truth', and Pilate still missed the point. Truth was standing in front of him and he couldn't see him; he was still looking for an 'it'. 'What is truth?' he asked almost cynically, as he turned away from a battered Jesus towards the screaming crowd to let them decide.

If Pilate were to stand in the marketplace today and ask the same question, he would probably receive blank stares. On the whole, the twenty-first century mind no longer searches for truth but for personal reality. We are encouraged to search for the hero inside ourselves and to follow our star, wherever it leads. I read an article in a leading newspaper which promoted replacing the ten commandments with the ten suggestions to provide a framework that would be more contemporary and relevant. The Bible is no longer the final authority; self and autonomous individualism are now the order of the day. If it is all right for me then it's all right and it has nothing to do with you. To declare absolute truth is to be narrow, judgemental and fundamentalist; each religion and philosophy is as valid as any other – as I heard one ex-member of the British royal family say, 'I choose a bit from each religion and put together my own, until I have something I am comfortable with.' This is the age of 'pick and mix' religion. Whatever I believe is just fine, as long as it makes me happy and what I do does not hurt anyone else.

We may think these ideas are new and all very postmodern, but they are not. They are as ancient as the hills – well as ancient as the garden anyway and I am sure there were hills in the garden. Way back in the beginning it was Satan who first challenged the authority and absolute nature of God. 'Did God really say?' he whispered in Eve's ear. Surely there is no absolute truth, no plumb line for right and wrong; surely God wouldn't want to put limits on you, by being so inflexible? With a little help from Einstein, Nietzsche and Darwin, the consensus of belief in God, initially challenged by Satan, would eventually be pushed aside. 'Move over God, we are in charge,' mankind would declare and Marx's plan would swing into

action. 'The debunking of religion must proceed all construc-
tive social change,' he announced, and all the 'isms' were born
– Communism, Marxism, Capitalism, Humanism, etc. However, 'isms' do not satisfy. Each may contain part of the truth,
but they are not *the* truth. Many of their adherents became
dissatisfied and moved on into the only thing they could be
sure of: 'Meism'.

So now we have created a world we can't handle. If God is
no longer in charge, then we are, and this control leads to huge
anxiety. We are responsible for maintaining the planet, and yet
instead of working with nature we have, on the whole, seen it
as a source of energy and raw materials to use for our own
devices and have all but conquered and destroyed it. As
someone has said: 'An apocalypse of exhaustion and conges-
tion seem imminent. We don't need bombs to run up mega
deaths, we just need our own stupidity.'

It is frightening living in a closed world which offers nothing
that deeply satisfies and locks each person into his own mind. I
know, I did it as a child. 'I think, therefore I am,' Descartes
famously concluded after he had set himself the task of
doubting everything in order that he might discover what was
really true. 'No,' says God, 'I AM therefore you are.'

Jehovah steps out of eternity into time, out of the Old
Testament into the New Testament and through the lips of his
son he offers the way back to himself: 'I am the way and the
truth and the life. No one comes to the Father except through
me' (Jn. 14: 6). It has always been that way, through the blood
shed in sacrifice and now through his blood shed on the cross.
Long after Darwin died, Jesus lives. Nothing has changed:

Without the way there is no going,
Without the truth there is no knowing,
Without the life there is no living.
'I am the way the truth and the life,'
That's what Jesus said.

The Samaritan woman had been stuck: not going anywhere, she had been confused; not understanding anything, she had been merely existing, but not living.

As Jesus stood before Pilate he made a simple statement: 'Everyone on the side of truth listens to me' (Jn. 18:37). Pilate made his choice and so did this woman: she listened. Not only did she listen but as her heart warmed she responded and cried out, when she heard she must worship in truth, 'I know Messiah is coming. When he comes, he will explain everything to us.' Or as Anne Graham Lotz says in her wonderful book with the same title, 'Just give me Jesus!'

She does not understand everything, but her heart is exploding as she recognises the truth being presented to her and in truth she worships him and reveals her need to him. 'I don't know everything and I have been waiting all my life for someone to come and fill in the gaps, to make it make sense, to rescue me from my confusion . . . He will explain everything.' I can only imagine the look of wonder and joy on her face as her outburst provokes the literally earth-shattering response: 'I AM speaks to you.' We will never know if she would have said anything else if the disciples had not come back at that moment, but in a sense there is nothing to say. She has found the one she has looked for in broken relationships and waited for in fumbling religion all her life and she is speechless. She leaves her pot. Jesus is now first in her life and she cannot wait to tell others and introduce them to the truth.

She has always known, as he pointed out to her, that she worshipped what she did not know and admits it by saying she is still waiting for someone to come and explain everything. The Samaritans only used part of the Old Testament and therefore their pick and choose approach meant that their worship was as limited as their understanding. The Jews were also limited by the very rituals that were put in place to release them and even though they thought they were in the right place to worship and on the right mountain, they had no connection with the real person of God and no understanding of what it meant to worship in truth.

'We are to more than understand truth about God; we are to encounter him.'[10] How do we know someone has had a personal encounter and really met God? We can hear it in what they say and see it in what they do. Jesus did not give out instructions on the truth about life and how to live it, he gave himself. He demanded personal contact. He looked at people and demanded they looked back so he could see the truth about them and they could receive the truth about him.

How amazing it must have been to walk the earth the same time as Jesus and to actually meet him. Along with the Samaritan woman, the woman who had been bleeding for twelve years and came to Jesus when she had tried everything and everyone else is one of my favourite women in the Bible. She tries to keep her distance. She touches only the edge of his cloak, thinking she can sneak away hidden in the crowd, and then, to her horror, she hears these words, 'Who touched me?' You can't expect to touch Jesus and not let him touch you. He is not a vending machine that dishes out what you need when you put a coin in the slot. He is a person and he demands a personal relationship from anyone who comes to him with a hungry heart, anyone who reaches out to him. If you are seeking, you will find, but you must allow yourself to be found. When you sidle into the back of the church hoping no one will see you and even worse, speak to you, he sees you, and like this woman you need to realise you cannot 'go by unnoticed'. How many seekers have tried to enter and exit a church anonymously only to discover, to their absolute amazement, that the preacher already seems to know all about them and is actually speaking straight to them. There might be hundreds of other people present, but the words are all being directed towards them! They thought they could hide in the crowd, but they have been spotted! He has seen them long before they have seen him and now he has got their attention for a moment, he has one or two things he wants them to know.

To realise we are known is the most wonderful discovery. It still leaves us amazed as it did the people in Jesus' day. When

Jesus saw Nathanael approaching, he said of him, 'Here is a true Israelite in whom there is nothing false.' 'How do you know me?' Nathanael asked. Jesus answered, 'I saw you while you were still under the fig tree before Philip called you.' Then Nathanael declared, 'Rabbi, you are the Son of God; you are the King of Israel' (Jn. 1:47–9).

You may think no one sees you standing in the shadows under a tree, or even hiding among the leaves, like Zacchaeus, up a tree, but God recognises a hungry heart. We have to come out from the shadows or down from the branches because he wants to come to our house, he wants personal contact, he wants a relationship. Jesus '*looked* at Simon', he '*saw* Matthew sitting', and long before she ever noticed him in the hazy heat of the day, he had probably been watching the Samaritan woman for quite a while as she dragged her weary body towards the well. Whenever Jesus *saw* someone he would ask a question or make a comment that would begin the personal connection with him. Whether they responded or not and actually *saw* him was up to them; he had made the first move. He would not only tell them the truth, he would give them the truth. In hearing and receiving his words, they would meet the living Word and they would receive God himself.

Jesus told the Jews who believed in him, 'If you hold to my teaching, you are really my disciples. Then you will know the truth and the truth will set you free' (Jn. 8:32). With our minds we understand what he teaches, with our spirits we respond to who he is and we are free to worship and to witness. I no longer *go* to the temple; my body *is* the temple of the Holy Spirit. I no longer *do* the sacrifice; I *am* the sacrifice. As Paul urges, '. . . offer your bodies as living sacrifices, holy and pleasing to God – this is your spiritual act of worship' (Rom. 12:1). My body is where I live. When I present it, I present both the inner me, who thinks and feels, and the outer me, who 'does' in response to the inner me! God wants me – the whole of me – mind, emotion, will and body presented in worship. If I am to worship in truth, then I need to understand the truth about the one I am worshipping and face the truth about who I am, surrendering my whole self to him. To surrender your broken self to God is a deeply personal and spiritual experience, but it is not a self-indulgent experience. The more we know of God, the more we want to know and the more we want to share our treasure with others.

I was once asked, on a radio programme, to tell the story of how I came to know God. When I had finished recalling my journey, which had included much searching, the interviewer leaned forward and said, 'And how did you know when you found God that he was *the* truth?' I didn't hesitate, 'I stopped looking,' I replied. 'That is how I knew he was *the* truth; there was no need to look for any other.' I had done far more than intellectually assent to a set of facts, I had met a person and he had set me free. Like the woman of Samaria, all I wanted to do was tell others. You don't have to understand everything about God to be changed by him. You don't have to know all there is to know to introduce others to him. You just have to have met him; you have to have faced the truth.

Chapter 10

Open Your Eyes and Look!

'I who speak to you am he.'

'I find it really hard to talk to people about Jesus.' How many times have you heard someone say these words or have you said them yourself? Most of us are not rushing into each day looking for opportunities to tell someone about Jesus because we think we don't know what to say and we have a sneaky feeling that even if we did, the majority of the folks whose paths cross ours, would not want to listen. We know that Jesus wants us to talk about him because he told us he did. The great commission, 'Go into all the world and make disciples', applies to you and me; there are no exceptions. To share the whole truth about Jesus, at some point we have to use words. It is no good just being 'nice' around people and hoping they will somehow 'catch' Jesus. Being nice may well encourage them to be more open, but in the end we must, 'always be prepared to give an answer to everyone who asks you to give the reason for the hope that you have' (1 Pet. 3:15).

Instead of seeing this as something threatening and to be avoided, unless absolutely necessary, we could see it as the most wonderful privilege on earth and find ourselves getting really excited about creating and seizing opportunities to share Jesus. Hopefully this chapter will show that it is not clever rhetoric that matters, but caring reality.

Let me show you how the question, 'How do I talk to people about Jesus?' is not a good place to start.

First, 'How do *I* . . .?' *You* are not the focus, *they* are, so to be thinking of how *you* will do whatever faces *you* is to have set off on the wrong tack. Directly before Peter says we must give a reasonable answer for the hope that is in us, he says, 'But in your hearts set apart Christ as Lord.' He comes first and if he has allowed us precious access into someone else's life then his agenda is of the utmost importance and number one on his agenda is the person who does not yet know him.

Second, 'talk to people'? It is very rare for God to lead us to people – plural. Most of us meet and talk to individuals rather than crowds. When we think of 'people' rather than a person, then the whole idea of saying anything seems very impersonal. Jesus himself rarely spoke to crowds, they often listened in as he was talking to his disciples or individuals, but his approach was 'won by one' and ours needs to be exactly the same.

Third, 'How do I talk?' Talking should not be our first concern; listening should. We do not blunder into someone's life with a set package of words paying no heed to what we see and hear of their particular circumstances. There is nothing worse than having a belief system parroted at you as if by rote. I remember two smartly dressed young men knocking on my door one day. I was busy with young children and it was not the best time to stop and chat, but as soon as I opened the door they launched into their well-honed spiel. There was no interest in me, my children, or anything other than saying what they had to say as fast as they could say it. Before long I was being offered a magazine about child-rearing. They had obviously heard the squawking going on in the background and realised this would be more appropriate for me than the one they carried on retirement, which I could see poking out of their bag. I felt very much intruded upon and even though I did not have the time, I was irritated, so I began to pick holes in some of the beliefs which were being so categorically thrust in my face. 'Well what we believe', the younger one said and began holding forth until his partner butted in and said, 'No we don't! That's not what we believe! What we believe is . . . ', and he took the argument on from there. I saw my opportunity and told them I needed to get back to my babes and suggested they sorted out what they believed before they knocked on people's doors in future. As I watched them walking down the road I saw the older one chastising the younger one for getting the script wrong and I felt sad that they believed in 'what' not 'who' and for their confusion.

Fourth, 'about Jesus'? As the above incident has just shown, when we think in terms of talking to someone *about* Jesus, rather than introducing someone *to* Jesus, then our approach will be factual and logical but probably detached and impersonal. We are sharing a person, not a belief system. There is a huge difference, as Jesus himself shows in John 4.

So, most of us have to admit that our starting point concerning the whole question of witnessing is flawed if we are saying, 'I find it really hard to talk to people about Jesus.' We may have been quietly patting ourselves on the back for admitting we find it hard, because at least we are showing that the thought has crossed our minds. The important thing, though, is that it has not taken its place in our hearts, and as long as we are motivated by a sense of duty, then any words that do come out of our mouths will fall dead on the floor. Let us move on and take part in what I can only describe as a master class on making disciples, conducted by Jesus Christ himself. Within a few verses and probably in less than an hour, Jesus has moved a woman from being an isolated outcast, with no confidence in herself and very little contact with anyone else, to being one of the most effective evangelists in the New Testament. How did he do it?

Jesus knew everything but only told a little.

Just to keep it simple and hopefully memorable, I have divided up his approach into sections all with headings starting with the letter 'L'. The pattern used with the woman at the well is repeated with several other strangers Jesus met and would seem to be particularly helpful with those individuals you meet just by 'chance'. Please do not think I am suggesting in any way that you arm yourself with a pattern and slap it on any poor unsuspecting individual you meet! The pattern is simply a set of principles which will only be appropriate and effective when inspired and applied by the Holy Spirit in his uniquely sensitive way.

Locate

John tells us that Jesus 'had to go through Samaria'. That was true for two reasons, one geographical and the other spiritual. Jesus was travelling from Judea in the south to Galilee in the north and unless he wanted to make a huge detour, then he had to go through Samaria. As we saw in an earlier chapter, most Jews avoided this area simply because they were so prejudiced they did not want to mix with Samaritans. But Jesus had spiritual reasons for finding himself in a particular geographical location. We are told in Proverbs, 'In all your ways acknowledge him and he will direct your paths', and that is exactly what Jesus did, all the time. He surrendered his own rights and desires and always put those of his father first. 'My food,' said Jesus, 'is to do the will of him who sent me and to finish his work' (Jn. 4:34).

'The one who sent me is with me; he has not left me alone, for I always do what pleases him' (Jn. 8:29). There was a woman in Samaria who needed to meet her God. There was a God in heaven who wanted her to meet his son and there was a son on earth who was willing to make the connection! God prompted Jesus to go to Samaria and for that reason, and that reason alone, he went. Why do I go where I go? Do I really believe that when I acknowledge God in all my ways he will direct my paths and wherever I find myself walking will not be an accident, but a special place to which I have been sent for a special assignment. I do not need to know in advance, I just need to set off with the assurance that he knows and all that happens is for his purposes.

To trust God implicitly and obey him wherever he sends me is both exciting and challenging. Sometimes he may direct me to places that others disapprove of and I will have to choose whose opinion matters most to me. I am sure Jesus' disciples muttered and grumbled about going into Samaria. What would people think? Never mind people, what did they honestly think? Maybe they would be contaminated by mixing with such people. Christians can be more judgemental than anyone else, piously pretending God may be offended, when really it is they themselves who are offended. If God prompts you to go somewhere, go and leave the fallout in his hands. God loves sinners but, so often, he can't get close to them because those who claim to be his children keep him to themselves and refuse to go where he wants to go in case he may be offended!! One of the things the religious people found most offensive about Jesus was his keenness not only to reach sinners, but also to party with them! When did you last offend the religious by hanging out with the wrong sort of people? When did you last lead someone to Christ?

When my husband was a student he spent a week in the heart of Manchester as part of a team who wanted to reach people with the good news about Jesus. After much door knocking, with very little response, he was becoming increasingly discouraged. One evening he was walking back to the place he was staying when he found himself passing a pub. 'Go inside' a voice within whispered. 'It's not so bad that I need a drink!' he heard himself saying, but the voice persisted, 'Go inside . . .'. My husband had not been brought up to go into pubs and the whole team would have been told it was definitely not the place they were expected to be seen hanging out! To cut a long story short, his legs did what his heart told them to, and he walked in to discover a very lonely young man, sitting at a table all by himself, drowning his sorrows in his beer and struggling to find the will to live. My husband was able to tell the man about Jesus and leave him to make his own response. Days later they 'happened' to meet on the street, and the man came to talk more about God and to say how much the encounter had meant to him.

There is a very interesting verse, a little later in John's Gospel, where Jesus says to his disciples, 'Whoever serves me must follow me: and where I am, my servant also will be' (Jn. 12:26). He takes the initiative and we fall into line. We don't decide where to go and who to talk to and then pray, 'Lord please be with me as I talk to this person.' Instead, we locate him in the driving seat in our lives, give him the director's chair and then get involved with his plans. 'Lord I see you are touching Jake's heart and speaking to him. Oh Lord, thank you for the privilege of allowing me to go and speak to him. Thank you for using my lips to say your words and allowing me to be a part of your plan and his life even though the rest of my family disapprove and think he lives in a bad part of town.' Never pretend you are protecting God when really you are protecting your own reputation: God is quite capable of protecting himself! Let him locate you wherever he may choose, to meet whomever he may choose, and you'll be amazed where you find yourself and what wonderful people you will meet there.

Look

As you read the woman at the well's story did you, along with Jesus, see a person or did you, along with the disciples, see a prostitute? What did you see?[11] Passion enables you to see a person with potential. Prejudice limits you to seeing a prostitute with problems. Long before you open your mouth, open your eyes and *look, look, look* at the person God has brought you into contact with. Each person is unique, but most of us are so quick to label and catagorise and in doing so stick a series of expectations or limitations on someone. We make huge leaps in our assumptions which were usually started by a simple observation about a nose ring or a hairstyle or certain clothes. If they wear one of those then they must obviously do drugs! To my shame I learnt this lesson through failure, which, if I am honest, is how I learn most of my lessons because God is firm and kind at the same time. He wants me to see where I have gone wrong, but he is too gracious to let me waste the mistake, he wants simply for me to learn from it.

One day, I was driving through the village where I went to church when I noticed someone I had never seen before standing on the side of the road waiting to cross it. I was in the car so I only had a fleeting impression, but it was enough for me to observe, assess and pass judgement. The man was in his twenties. He had long hair in a ponytail and wore a tatty T-shirt, a faded denim jacket, black leather pants and scuffed black boots; he had a child standing beside him holding his hand. I had had time to take in the child's appearance too, which was easy because he was almost the double of his father; his hair and clothes were identical, except that he had jeans on instead of leathers. As I sped past I remember thinking, 'I bet he was a biker and a 'has been' into heavy rock. How wrong of him to impose that image on to such a young child. I bet the child didn't want that ponytail and his father made him have it.' They were labelled and pigeonholed and my prejudiced eyes had failed to see their wonderful potential. If I had listened to my heavenly father I would have heard him whisper, 'I am their heavenly father too.' But prejudice does not listen, it is too busy piling up its proud assumptions.

I did not give them a second thought. I did not need to. I had applauded myself for being so discerning and moved on, to church the next day as it so happened. I was sitting on the front row and as the service ended I turned in my seat to greet familiar and hopefully unfamiliar faces. There weren't often many of those and it was always good to see new people come into a service. Who should be sitting on the back row – I am sure by now you have guessed – but that familiar, unfamiliar face with the ponytail and the little boy next to him. My eyes darted along the row and saw another little boy, a toddler wriggling around on the knee of someone who I guessed was the mum. As I think back to that day and try and remember what she was wearing, I can't: I had learnt my lesson! I shot out of my seat and went over to meet them. I have to admit that as I got closer I did notice that she had a nose stud and thought how beautiful it looked. We talked, they had just moved into the village. Their son would be starting new at the school and would be in the same class as my son. I asked if they would like to get together before term started and there began a wonderful friendship for my son and for me. Ellie is still one of my dearest friends and is one of the most refreshingly godly people I know. I am so glad they chose to walk into my church and not allow prejudice to prevent them from mixing with folks who behave and dress in a different way from the way they do. (By the way, Ben later had his ponytail which he, not his dad, had wanted, cut off because he found the children at school were mean to him about it and the nurse thought he was a girl; sadly prejudice starts very young.)

We cannot know for sure, but it is possible that the disciples had passed the woman as they went into the village to buy food. We know that the well was outside the village and as she was coming from it and they were going to it, their paths may have momentarily crossed. Why did they not stop her and get into conversation with her? They simply did not *see* her. They may well have seen a Samaritan woman shuffling along in the heat of the day, but what was that to them? They were hungry, their need was so important that it blinded them to anyone else's. We can be so selfish and so selective about who we choose to witness to. As long as it doesn't disrupt our schedule, doesn't delay us or lead us off track, then we may throw in a few words for Jesus. My will is to do my will and woe betide anyone who gets in the way.

How different Jesus' approach is. We are told he is tired from the journey. No doubt he is also hungry like the disciples and he is definitely thirsty because he asks the woman for a drink. When you are tired, hungry and thirsty are you open to introducing someone to Jesus, knowing it may well take a long time and you are going to get more tired, more hungry and more thirsty? Reason would tell you to be sensible, be practical, you must keep yourself fit and healthy or you will be no good to anyone. See to your own needs first and then you will be able to look to the needs of others. Not so.

One of the wonderful things I have learnt, when I talk to strangers about God, is that your needs can be the very thing that opens up conversation rather than preventing it happening. No one wants to talk to anyone who has got it all together. If you are willing to be open about your need, your hurt, whatever it is that is crying out the loudest in you at that moment, then your very vulnerability can allow someone to expose their vulnerability. I can remember years ago my sister, who was very anti-God at the time, was sitting on a train when the girl beside her suddenly burst into tears. Jane did not know what to say, but she did not turn her back and must have looked concerned because she suddenly heard the girl starting to explain her tears: 'I am so sorry,' she said, 'but I have just been to a my mother's funeral and I am really upset. I know I don't need to be because I know my mother has gone to heaven and I believe in God too but I didn't want to lose my mother when I am so young.' Through her sobs she went on to talk about how much both God and her mother meant to her and then seeing Jane was about to get off and feeling she had not done a very good job, she thrust a book entitled, *The Singer*, into her hand saying, 'This will make it all a lot clearer to you.' *The Singer*, turned out to be an allegory about Jesus, which, if you understood it, was absolutely beautiful, but if you did not or did not want to, as Jane did not, at that point in her life, it was very confusing. It was passed on to me and I was so encouraged, as a young Christian, that in a situation where someone would have every reason to wrap themselves in their grief, a young woman had been so in touch with God that she had used her need to soften the heart of someone who was soon to start her own search for him. Jane did not understand

'The Singer' for a long time, but she did recognise unselfish love when she saw it. Even through her tears and personal pain and need this girl had looked and *seen* the need of the person next to her, a person who to the casual onlooker may have looked very 'cool', but who deep down in her heart was very fearful of death.

When you meet a stranger look for clues that will show you who they really are, not for evidence to confirm your judgement of who you have already decided they are. Why do they really pierce their body? Is it simply a fashion statement or do they have low self-esteem? Are they making an angry gesture? Who has made them angry? Why do their shoulders droop? What burdens do they carry? What makes that glimmer of a smile cross their lips? Is it cynicism? Where did it come from in one so young? When did they get hurt and have to build protective walls around themselves? Why does that leg never stop jigging up and down? What are they so nervous about? (That is a genuine one – I am not pretending! Even a jigging leg can lead into a conversation about God.) I know, I encountered one when I sat beside a young man in his twenties for six hours as we both waited for cancellation slots to take a driving test. 'Well,' you say 'It is obvious why his leg was jigging if you were waiting for driving tests!' Not for six hours! Once I realised we were there for the duration I thought, 'OK God, this appointment is about far more than meeting an examiner, this is all about this guy next to me, so over to you.' I looked, I listened and after five and a half hours, now knowing this young man's parents were divorced, his mother lived in England, his brother had money lavished on him that he never saw, etc., etc., I was able to introduce him to the whole idea of peace, purpose and love all found in the person of Jesus. When we parted I didn't care whether I passed the test or not, and I had tried to show him that in the light of eternity it was not such a big deal whether he passed or not, but I think on that score I was pushing it! It's hard to focus on eternity when the present is so pressing!

Just as there is a whole world behind people's gestures and we must look beyond the obvious if we are going to see who they really are, so there is a long story behind their words and if we are to understand anything of who the person before us is, we must . . .

Listen

Because Jesus is far more aware of the woman's real need than she is, he is able to lead her very naturally in their conversation to the point when she realises that need and cries out for an answer. If he had gone barging in saying, 'Well it's obvious what your problem is', the conversation would have died on the spot. Instead Jesus patiently and discerningly listens for her true story behind the words. He does not avoid her comments but expands and explores them. She tries to pick a quarrel over religious matters, to avoid talking about her personal hurts and concerns, and he slowly but surely leads her to answer questions she has not even acknowledged she is asking. You may well come up with more thoughts as you look at the text, but from my observation it seems Jesus has a hidden script.

'The purposes of a man's heart are deep waters, but a man of understanding draws them out' (Prov. 20:5). What a wonderful title for Jesus: 'A man of understanding'. Watch how he draws answers to the following in such a short time:

What do you spend most of your life doing? Filling my water pot.
Does that satisfy you? No.
Why do you come to the well alone and at noon? Because I am hurting.
What hurts you most? Prejudice.
Are you hiding something? Yes.
What are you most ashamed of? Failed relationships.
What do you believe about God? I am not sure, I am confused.
Where did you get your ideas about God from? The fathers.
Does what you believe satisfy you? No. I feel detached from it all. It is just what I have been told.

Do you think it is possible to be satisfied? Yes, one day when the Messiah comes.
Are you waiting for him? Yes.
Would you like the Messiah to come now? Oh yes.
I who speak to you am he.

She didn't actually say any of these words, but in their discussion about water pots, religion and hidden husbands, Jesus heard them and is able to reflect back to her what she has probably been unwilling to admit to for years. What a relief to be understood, particularly when you feel so misunderstood by those around you. What a relief to be listened to and not condemned. What a relief to be loved and received and what a relief to realise the Messiah himself is speaking to you, he has heard your heart's cry and he is the answer to your every longing, your every question, your every hurt, and your every need. It is time to put down that pot: life is just beginning.

Learn

Sometimes people who talk to others about God give the impression they know it all and are not willing to learn anything from the person they are talking, not listening, to. As I was preparing this chapter, I was interrupted by the doorbell. It was cold and snowy and the man who had rung the bell looked rather flustered and windswept.

'I am sorry to bother you,' he said, 'but can I have a moment of your time?'

Before I had time to say Yes or No, he was off again.

'It's not easy for me to do this. When I was younger I was so shy I couldn't even talk on the telephone.'

'Oh.'

'When you look around the world don't you think it is in an awful mess?'

'Well, Yes I suppose . . .'

'One day God is going to come and there is going to be a new world. Don't you think it is important to think about God?'

'Well, actually . . .'

'I have a book here I would like you to look at.' (Fumbling in his bag.)

'The thing is, I know Jesus.' (Addressed to the top of the head still fumbling in the bag.)

'Ah here it is. I would like you to look at this.'

'But I know I can have peace with God now through his Holy Spirit. I don't want to wait until the end of the age.'

'Here, it says here . . .' (pointing to a text, not having heard a word I was saying.)

'I am sorry, I don't want your book.' I wanted to show him that since he had not been willing to learn anything from me, I was having a hard time being willing to learn anything from him. But before I got the words out I heard,

'Oh. Goodbye then and thank you for your time.'

What did that man learn about me? Nothing except that I didn't want his book. He did not know why I did not want his book. My husband could just have committed suicide and my life could have been totally falling apart for all he knew. He was not willing to learn, only to 'teach'. Jesus, who knew everything anyway, was still willing to learn from what the woman was willing to disclose and what she was trying to hide, exactly where she was coming from. Of course he told her things, but only after he had listened, learnt and been willing to . . .

Linger

The man at my door rushed me. I know he was cold and I could have invited him in, but I doubt if he would have come because he was obviously in a hurry to 'do' a certain number of houses by lunch time. There is nothing worse than trying to piece your thoughts together and share them with someone who keeps looking at their watch. You can't share your heart in a hurry.

Jesus lets the woman at the well know that he is not going to go rushing off by asking her for a drink. It would have taken a while for her to lift the well lid, lower the bucket, pull it back up and scoop out the drink, which presumably he would not have bolted down in one gulp. He was always willing to invest time in someone in need, making them feel that for however long it took, they were the most important person in the world. They felt they were because they were! 'Oh,' you say, 'I am too busy to be side-tracked by interruptions in my day. That was his job – Jesus came to meet people and that is what he did.' Jesus was also busy, but never rushed. One day he was responding to a crisis. Jairus' daughter was dying and Jairus pleaded with Jesus to come to his house. Jesus set off towards the house, but he did not put a flashing light on his head and switch a siren on, he steadily made his way through the crowds until, in the midst of the crush, he felt someone touch his cloak. He could have ignored it, knowing he had more pressing things to deal with, but he didn't, he lingered. The woman, who had touched him, was called out of the crowd. She was healed. She left in peace (amazing in the midst of all the noise and turmoil, but captured in that little bubble of suspended time in an encounter with the eternal one) and Jesus carried on only to find Jairus' daughter had died in the delay. But Jesus was about his father's business and because he was prepared to pause, both the woman and then the daughter were healed.

How different our day would look if we set out wondering what people God was going to bring across our paths and we recognised them, when they arrived, instead of seeing them as an inconvenience. It is so easy to convince ourselves that the busier we are, the more important we are. How pleased we feel when a friend calls and obviously needs to talk and we hear ourselves saying, 'I'd love to see you. I can fit you in for coffee a week on Wednesday.' We think we have achieved something doubly clever. Firstly, they will be impressed by our hectic schedule and secondly they will feel very special because they are allowed a little slot in it. Rubbish! They will probably decline the offer, put down the phone and try and find someone else who is a little more discerning, a lot less selfish and who actually knows the meaning of the word . . .

Love

Time equals Love. To say you love someone and then not be willing to spend any time with them would be ridiculous. When you love someone and give them your time you give them a sense of dignity because you are making them your highest priority. The very fact that Jesus was willing to take time with the woman said to her, loud and clear, 'You matter.' It was probably a very long time since anyone had said those words to her. Before she was willing to hear what this man was saying she needed to trust him and it was probably a very long time since she had done that too. Jesus loved her as she was, but he loved her too much to leave her as she was and therefore he was not put off by her initial defensiveness. His whole approach is summed up in Paul's wonderful description of love in 1 Corinthians 13:4–8:

Love is patient,	*Jesus lingers.*
love is kind.	*'Will you give me a drink?'*
It does not envy, it does not boast,	*'If you knew the gift of God . . .'*
it is not proud	*'. . . you would have asked him.'*
It is not rude, it is not self-seeking,	*'but whoever drinks the water I give him . . .'*
it is not easily angered,	*'Are you greater than our father, Jacob? . . . Everyone who drinks this water will be thirsty again.'*
it keeps no record of wrongs.	*'If you knew . . . you would have asked.'*

Love does not delight in evil,	*'You are right when you say . . .'*
but rejoices with the truth.	*'What you have just said is quite true.'*
It always protects,	*'. . . whoever drinks the water I give him will never thirst.'*
always trusts, always hopes,	*'. . . the water I give him will become in him a spring of water welling up to eternal life.'*
always perseveres.	*'Believe me woman, a time is coming . . .'*
Love never fails.	*'I who speak to you am he.'*

How could she not feel loved after a conversation like this? Jesus has gone at her pace, listened to her deepest needs, only responded to what she actually says and only revealed the truth about himself when she was very obviously ready to hear it. 'When he comes he will explain everything to us.' Her longing is palpable, her thirst can no longer be hidden and it is time for Jesus to reveal himself. 'Perfect love casts out fear.' Her barriers are down, the religious discussions have come to an end and she is now open to the relationship that he is longing to offer her.

Leave

Leave people with Jesus and just Jesus. You may have told them your story, you may have wandered through various beliefs, you may have listened to their confusion as they pieced together their story, but in the end, it is the person of Jesus Christ you are introducing them to and whom they need to be left with. Clever arguments may impress a person, however, it is only when they are personally confronted with the question 'Who do you say that I am?' that a person will realise that they are accountable to him, not you, not their fathers, not those who sit in judgement on their lives, but to him.

You do not have to understand everything to begin a relationship with Jesus. It is not given to you as a reward for getting top marks in a theology test. You simply have to take that first tentative step which says, I'm beginning to trust and want to trust more, I believe and want to believe more, I know a little and want to know more. Your faith only needs to be as small as a mustard seed and you are on your way: 'Then, leaving her water jar, the woman went back to the town and said to the people, "Come, see a man who told me everything I ever did. Could this be the Christ?" ' (Jn. 4:28–9).

The woman knew a little and told her everything she knew! The minute the woman at the well had an inkling of the truth she was off to tell others. Her witness was simple but incredibly effective, not because it was clever or even complete, but because it was real. Look at her approach, I won't call it strategy, because she had not had time to formulate one, she just set off and showed what an amazingly fast learner she was.

She puts God first

Her water pot still needs filling, but who cares! Eternal matters are far more important than the immediate. I love this woman! She could have gone home, had a good think about everything she had heard, made the dinner, tried to think of someone she could talk to and having realised there was no one, never set foot out of the door! But she does not; she has met the Messiah, the one she has been waiting for all her life, through all the boring sermons she has heard, in all the failed relationships she has experienced, and she can't wait to tell the world. It would have been so easy at this point to find a stranger to talk to who did not know all about her. Maybe this was such a small community that there were no strangers and she did not know anyone she did not know! Whatever the reason, she sets off and goes to the hardest place of all: the town which has known her and ostracised her.

She puts people first

She knows all her neighbours have the same limited knowledge of God that she has, they suffer under the same burden of prejudice that all Samaritans experienced and they need to know there is a man who can set them free. It is not easy to witness to those who know you and to go to the place where everyone knows all your failure and weakness. But remember, you are not going to talk about you, you are going to introduce them to him. Those who have just enough religion to make them respectable will no doubt be the hardest to approach but, if you avoid giving your opinions or pretending you know more than you do, they will be introduced to the Truth himself through the truth of your experience and words: 'They said to the woman, "We no longer believe just because of what you said; now we have heard for ourselves, and we know that this man really is the Saviour of the world" ' (Jn. 4:41–2).

She puts Jesus first

This woman is a link in the chain, maybe even the weakest link; she is not the chain. Having introduced the villagers to Jesus she is willing to step out of the way and let them find their way towards him by themselves. If someone is hungry and seeking they will keep seeking long after you have sown a seed in their thinking. You can 'water' their every step through prayer but you do not need to be there, holding their hand along the way. How freeing and how exciting! As we left England and moved to Canada, both my daughter and I left friends whose grasp of God was very tentative. Were we abandoning them? Would they fall away because we weren't there to answer their every question and coax them on their way? Not a bit of it! Since we have left they have both come to know Jesus in a much deeper way all by themselves. They have had choices to make and have found themselves accountable to him. They have had questions to ask and have found the answers in his word, directly from him. Maybe God even needed us to get out of the way so they could see him clearly for themselves without us blocking the view!

She puts herself last

The Samaritan woman could well have been immobilised by shame and guilt about her past, but instead she uses it as a springboard to her present joy. 'He told me everything I ever did' is her main witnessing statement. Pain and failure do not disqualify you from witnessing, on the contrary they make your words valid. You are not saying, 'I have it all sorted', you are saying, 'I need Jesus and you need Jesus and so as two needy people we have lots to talk about.' Personal pain is a pathway into the real world of any feeling person you meet. They don't snicker and say, 'Well we could have told him everything you ever did!' I think they are so amazed at her freedom and lightness of step, which has come from meeting the one who really knows her, that they can't wait to meet this amazing person who has brought about the change. Psalm 142:7 says, 'Set me free from my prison that I may praise your name.' As this woman bursts from her prison, so the words about her rescuer pour forth from her mouth and they are hard to resist.

She also allows them to go further in their understanding than she has gone. She approaches them saying, 'Could this be . . . ?' She has questions and doubts, which she willingly admits to. They eventually conclude, 'We know he really is . . .', with a certainty after two days in his presence that she did not have after less than an hour. I only hope she was part of the group who sat listening and 'because of his words . . . became believers'. Her tentative start and initial approach bring these Samaritans to the point where they can make not just one of the most amazing statements in the Bible, but one of the most amazing statements in all of history: '. . . this man really is the Saviour of the world'. That includes all of us, even Samaritans who had been pushed out by the chosen people for so long. Jesus is *the* way and *the* truth and the woman of Samaria enabled a whole village – her whole world – to discover that for themselves, as they met him for themselves. What an evangelist!

Maybe it was the fact that the disciples had not yet grasped this fundamental truth which made them such ineffectual witnesses in contrast with the woman:

The disciples knew a lot about Jesus and didn't tell anybody anything! In the school of witnessing, they were definitely at the bottom of the class, and Jesus had to gently, but very firmly, take them on one side and go back to basics.

They failed to make God's work their priority

While the woman was abandoning her water pot and ignoring physical needs the disciples were still wittering on about the need to eat. First they missed the woman because they were too intent on heading off to town to get food and then they missed her again, on their return, because they were so concerned about getting Jesus to eat the food they have just brought from the town,

> Just then his disciples returned and were surprised to find him talking to a woman. But no one asked, 'What do you want?' or 'Why are you talking with her?'
>
> Then, leaving her water jar, the woman went back to the town and said to the people, 'Come, see a man who told me everything I ever did. Could this be the Christ?" They came out of the town and made their way toward him.
>
> Meanwhile his disciples urged him, 'Rabbi, eat something' (Jn. 4:27–31).

By now, most of the inhabitants of the town are making their way towards the well and they just don't see them. They are still blind. 'Then his disciples said to each other, "Could someone have brought him food?" '

> We get what we go after in life. The disciples were interested in food. They went into the village to get food. They came back with it. The Lord was interested in souls. He was interested in saving men and women from sin, and giving them the water of everlasting life. He, too, found what he went after. What are we interested in?[12]

Time for a visual aid from the master teacher because . . .

They failed to see what was under their noses

Perhaps they were surrounded by corn fields and Jesus simply directs their attention to them or perhaps, as Anne Graham Lotz imaginatively suggests, all the villagers making their way up the hill, with their robes blowing in the breeze, looked like rows of corn and Jesus simply tells them to 'open their eyes and look.' If the disciples' prejudice prevented them from believing that Samaritans could receive eternal life then they would not have expected to see a harvest in the fields in Samaria. Never write a whole group of people off and refuse to get in among them. Jesus put himself right in the middle of the Samaritans' need and met one needy lady. The disciples remained on the edge of the very obvious need and met nobody. Hells Angels can be saved. Prostitutes can be saved. I know people who work within both these groups ready to meet individuals and introduce them to the Saviour of the whole world.

They failed to recognise ripe fruit

It is all too easy to be full of good intentions and achieve nothing. I do not think the disciples were actually planning any harvest, but in his graciousness, Jesus gives them the benefit of the doubt. 'Do you not say, "Four months more and then the harvest"? I tell you, open your eyes and look at the fields! They are ripe for harvest' (Jn. 4:35). James McDonald has said that too many of us wait around spending years of nurturing and fertilizing green apples that will never go red, when we ought to be concentrating on identifying the red apples and picking them. There are always people ready, pick them and don't keep putting off what God wants by saying, 'We'll just wait four months more.'

They failed to be a link in the chain

Jesus made it very clear to the disciples that he had a specific job for them to do and they had missed it. 'I sent you to reap what you have not worked for. Others have done the hard work and you have reaped the benefits of their labour' (Jn. 4:38). If you try to do someone else's job, or indeed do nothing, then you will be tempted to give up when you see nothing happen. Each of us is asked to finish what God gives us to do and then move on. Of course if we never even start, because we are always waiting for the harvest, then we will never finish and we will never know the wonderful satisfaction of being in the right place at the right time simply to point someone to Jesus. What an amazing privilege and what a huge responsibility. All it takes is someone willing to open their eyes and look and be willing then simply to set off and see. And that leads us to our final chapter.

Chapter 11

Set Off and See

*'. . . leaving her water jar the woman went
back to the town . . .'*

When life ceases to be an adventure, it ceases to be life and
becomes simply existence. What is an adventure? In my
understanding it is when you embark on something not
knowing what the outcome is going to be. That may well be an
African Safari or it may well be a trip to the local supermarket
to see if the tomatoes are on offer and you can afford them. A
day with no element of surprise is a dull day and however old
you are I am convinced it is imperative to retain a spirit of
adventure to stay alive.

When I first met my husband he was more adventurous than
I and probably still is. I soon realised I would have to get on
board or I would get left behind. We would be heading up
someone's private drive to have a look at their mansion and I
would always be saying, 'Do you think we ought to be doing
this? What if we get caught?' In his mind that would only add
to the adventure and he had his well-rehearsed excuses all
ready anyway!

Between them, God and my husband have taught me to 'Set
off and see' and I am extremely thankful to both! When you
live within the realm of the 'allowed' and the 'safe' you attempt
to retain total control. When you step into the realm of the
unknown, you have the chance of seeing God at work in the

most amazing ways, and you move from having a detached, boring religion to having a very exciting relationship with the Creator of the Universe who made adventure possible in the first place when he set the world spinning in space and hung planets tantalisingly close, but mostly just out of reach.

In this last chapter I want to explore the principal of being willing to 'Set off and see' which the Samaritan woman had so obviously grasped, right off the bat! I am sure that for her meeting Jesus must have seemed like the end of a very long journey. In many ways it was, but it was also the beginning of a new journey. I cannot remember where I read the following illustration and if you recognise it as yours, please forgive me for using it with no acknowledgement and thank you for it! It goes something like this: 'Those who have a religion stand under the lamp post and dare not step outside the boundary of the shed circle of light. Those who have a relationship have a light in their hand; they can go wherever they are led and light will always be shed on the path ahead.'

Jesus did not just say, 'I am the light of the world'; he also said, 'You are the light of the world.' Once you have received the Holy Spirit into your life, you have the light of Christ within and it is his light that shines without. It is time to step out from huddling in the security of the little pool of light at the base of the lamp post, with all its limitations, and go out on the road with Jesus – what an adventure!

The woman at the well had not come to draw water with any sense of adventure, simply dead drudgery and routine. However, she had met the living water and as she received that living water (which we would come to know as the Holy Spirit once Jesus had ascended into heaven), she discovered the truth of what he had just told her. 'Everyone who drinks this water will be thirsty again, but whoever drinks the water I give him [I am sure he really meant 'her' and someone wrote 'him'!] will never thirst. Indeed, the water I give him [same applies!] will become in him [and again] a spring of water welling up to eternal life' (Jn. 4:13–14). She would not have been present, a little while later, when Jesus explained publicly what he had previously shared very personally and privately with her:

> On the last and greatest day of the Feast, Jesus stood and said in a loud voice, 'If a man is thirsty, let him come to me and drink. Whoever believes in me, as the Scripture has said, streams of living water will flow from within him.' By this he meant the Spirit, whom those who believed in him were later to receive. Up to that time the Spirit had not been given, since Jesus had not been glorified (Jn. 7:37–9).

She was no doubt still busy letting him 'bubble up' from within her, to share with anyone where adventure with God may lead her to.

One step leads to another and by believing (He is the Truth), receiving (He is the Life), and proceeding (He is the Way), she is embarking on an adventure which ensures that neither she, nor any of those she meets, will never be the same again. The simple words, 'leaving her water jar, the woman went back to the town and said to the people . . .', give no clue as to how daunting that short journey must have been. It can be much harder to go back than to go forward, because when we retrace our steps, we are admitting that that was where life got difficult and we maybe took a wrong turn, leaving behind some unfinished issues. Before you get all excited about heading off on a new adventure with God, listen carefully to him: he may be asking you to go back before you go on. Perhaps you have a broken relationship which needs to be given the chance to heal. Perhaps you have an incomplete task that needs finishing. Perhaps you have an unforgiven sin that needs confessing. Perhaps you have a command from God, which you know you heard long ago and now it needs obeying. Do not be discouraged: you are in good company. Before we take a look at those who knew God and who were willing to 'Set off and see', let us linger patiently for a moment, as God did, with those who were not going anywhere until they had gone back.

One of the characters in the Bible who pulls at my heartstrings the most is Hagar, maid to Sarah and surrogate mother of Abraham's child. We do not have time to go into her story in detail, but suffice it to say she had a very raw deal. She was told to bear a child for her master and having done so, she was rejected by her mistress. Not surprisingly all she wants to do is run away. This she does, heading off to the desert where she hopes no one will find her. There is no place on earth to hide from your loving heavenly Father and without delay he sends the angel of the Lord to draw alongside her. Knowing how painful the situation was for Hagar, but also knowing how impossible it would be for her to survive in the desert and wanting to protect her and the baby, he says to her, 'Go back to your mistress and submit to her' (Gen. 16:9).

The road back is a long one and she knows further suffering awaits her at the end of it so why is she willing to go? Simply because she has had a personal encounter with God. 'I have now seen the one who sees me' (Gen. 16:13), she bravely declares and so I will go back knowing I am not alone. God has not changed the situation, but he has changed her perspective of the situation. Whatever her mistress does to her, or says to her, she has a secret in her heart which will sustain her, and it is this: God loves me, and has plans for me and therefore I dare go back. 'God can do wonders with a broken heart if you give him all the pieces.'[13] A journey back may well involve the pain of surrendering the broken things in your life which, until you do, will be strewn like broken pottery across your path, hindering and preventing any real progress and certainly excluding you from the adventure he has planned for you, because it simply hurts too much each time you attempt to set off.

Another person God had to go looking for in the desert, because he had run away in fear, was his servant, Elijah. After a spectacular confrontation with the prophets of Baal, on the top of Mount Carmel, when Elijah had put both his and God's reputation on the line, the triumphant Elijah is crushed by the wicked words of one woman and he legs it! How could someone who had been so brave suddenly become so cowardly? He forgot that this was God's fight and not his and when all his strength ran out, so did he! While Elijah hid at the back of a cave God put on one of the most amazing sound and light shows in Scripture, just to remind him of his power, and then with his gentle whisper, he drew him out of the cave and reminded him he was not on his own and there was still work to do.

Elijah had started to think he had the lead role in the drama and he had got stage fright. Once God had re-established that he was not only the author, but also the leading man, then Elijah was willing to do what he said and to go back. Or as F. B. Meyer so succinctly put it, 'To resume the forsaken work and to retake the abandoned post.'[14] From this point on what Elijah did was never so spectacular. He went back to encourage the school of the prophets and to train his successor, Elisha. But God, with his amazing sense of fun and adventure, did give him the lead role just fleetingly one more time, as he starred in *Chariots of Fire* and went to heaven in a way no person has ever done before or since. Who thinks walking with God is not an adventure! Thankfully, we never know what is about to happen.

> As they were walking along talking together, suddenly a chariot of fire and horses of fire appeared and separated the two of them, and Elijah went up to heaven in a whirlwind. Elisha saw this and cried out, 'My father! My father! The chariots and horsemen of Israel!' And Elisha saw him no more. Then he took hold of his own clothes and tore them apart (2 Kgs. 2:11–12).

Strange, but then you can't blame the 'old fellow', I mean what would you have done? Just stood there and said, 'Way to go Elijah!'? What an adventure and one he would never have known if he had not been willing to come out of the cave of fear and doubt and go back when God gently told him to.

Before we leave those who were sent back, I can't resist looking at the man who tried to escape God's adventure and in doing so ended up having the ride of his life, a whale of a time and an adventure which far surpassed the one God had originally planned. Yes, you guessed it – Jonah. When God told Jonah to go to Nineveh and preach to the city, he caught the first boat going in the opposite direction that he could find. Just as God can find you in the desert, so he can track you down on the high seas and if he chooses, make them so high that your fellow sailors, realising you are the problem, decide to chuck you overboard. Being swallowed by a 'great fish' and spending three days and nights sloshing around in its belly, before being vomited onto dry ground, would be enough to bring most of us to our senses, but not Jonah.

He did go back and do what God had told him to do but he did not go 'ready for anything' (as my friend has as her motto); he still had his own ideas about how things should work out and therefore reserved the right to his own opinion when they didn't. We are to obey and leave the consequences in God's hands. He obeyed and then went and sat under a vine and sulked about the consequences. When the people repented in response to his message he was angry with God for being so kind and compassionate with them. When a little worm nibbled away at his vine, he was angry about his disintegrated parasol. It was then that God stepped in and showed him how selfish and hard-hearted he was being. When God sends us back he does not want us to be just obedient, he wants us to be willing. You cannot be willful and willing at the same time. It is 'self' that keeps the 'ful' bit full and though it may not exclude you from being involved in God's adventure, it will certainly rob you of the joy which recognises God at work in the fish, the foliage and if you could only see it, your little friend, the worm.

Although I may have dealt with these three characters in a somewhat frivolous way, the principal they demonstrate is far from frivolous; on the contrary it is absolutely fundamental if we are going to move from having a religion to believe in, to having a relationship with a God we can trust. Trust is the way *into* the Christian life, as we put our trust in the one who died on the cross so our sins may be forgiven, and it is also the way *through* the Christian life. Daily, God asks us to go into situations which are confusing, challenging and often overwhelming. If we do not trust him, we will never set off in the first place and if we do not continue to trust him we will find ourselves in over our heads and wanting to quit, just as Elijah did.

We are not always presented with a clear command as Jonah was, and therefore a choice about whether to set off in the first place. Many of us find ourselves being beckoned down a road, from which there is no escape, however frightening the road may look. As we step towards what we perceive as the inevitable, the God of surprises has the opportunity to intervene and reveal that he is in fact the God of the impossible.

Remember Shadrach, Meshach and Abednego? Refusing to bow down to the statue Nebuchadnezzar had set up of himself, they were told they were to be thrown into a blazing furnace. There was a chink in their courageous response and to me it shows a greater degree of trust than if there had been no chink at all.

'O Nebuchadnezzar, we do not need to defend ourselves before you in this matter. If we are thrown into the blazing furnace, the God we serve is able to save us from it, and he will rescue us from your hand, O king.' Fighting talk up to this point. Now listen to their little qualification: 'But even if he does not, we want you to know, O king, that we will not serve your gods or worship the image of gold you have set up' (Dan. 3:16–18). They may not have been one hundred per cent sure of their God, but they were one hundred per cent sure there was no other and so they were willing to 'Set off and see', and what an amazing sight, not only they, but also the awful spectators saw. Having bound and tied the three men and heated the furnace so hot that it fried the men who pushed them in, the king could not believe what happened next.

Look! I see four men walking around in the fire, unbound and unharmed, and the fourth looks like a son of the gods. . . . Come out! Come here! Praise be to the god of Shadrach, Meshach and Abednego . . . They trusted in him and defied the king's command and were willing to give up their lives rather than serve or worship any god except their own God (Dan. 3:25, 26, 28).

Did you notice those two words, 'willing' and 'trusted'? What an incredible outcome. Not only did their willingness and trust lead to a close encounter with who we can only assume is Jesus, long before he was ever born, but it also caused a pagan king to praise the only true God for the first time in his life. A few chapters later we find another king, Darius, unwillingly throwing Daniel into the lions' den, for defying his decree, with these tentatively trusting words: 'May your God whom you serve continually, rescue you!' (Dan. 6:16). And you know the story – he did! 'And when Daniel was lifted from the den, no wound was found on him, because he had trusted in his God' (Dan. 6:23). There it is again – the trust, without which they would never have got into the situation which led them into being thrown into the furnace and the lions' den in the first place and with which they all experienced the most remarkable deliveries. Have you ever been rescued by God? If not then it could well be that you have never trusted him enough to step into a situation which you would then have to trust him to get you out of!

'OK' you are thinking, 'then that excludes me, I shall never trust enough to step into a furnace without a fire-proof blanket wrapped around me. I have too many doubts.' 'Doubts?' did I hear you say? 'God has adventures for doubters too. They are also called simply to 'Set off and see.' Doubt never disqualifies you from playing a part in God's drama. We don't have to delve too far to find such a character, in fact only into a wine-press where he was hiding to thresh his wheat. Having been called 'mighty warrior' and told to go in the strength he had, to defeat the Midianites, Gideon feels it only polite to admit to the somewhat mistaken angel of the Lord, who was making these wild claims for him, that he felt neither mighty nor strong. Although God promises him at that point, 'I will be with you', it takes a lot of patience on God's part and a lot of fun and games on Gideon's with a wet and dry fleece, for him to be convinced enough in God's faithfulness in the present to be able to trust it in the future. Against all the odds and in the most unconventional manner, with empty jars and torches and a woefully inadequate fighting force, Gideon does eventually set off and see that he might be fighting the fight, but it is God who wins the battle.

Someone has said, 'Attempt great things for God; expect great things of God.' How many of us attempt even tiny things? How many of us set out into each day with no real expectation of God being remotely interested in our little lives and therefore not even considering that he may be interested in the lives of those who also populate our day. I have found, in my own life, that when I set off with a prayerful sense of expectation, then I go through the day with anticipation and usually it is not disappointed.

Recently I flew to England for a short holiday and then back to Canada. When I arrived at check-in for the outward leg of my journey, to my horror I discovered, with a little help from the girl at the desk, that my tickets were all for the date of the day before. I had come a day late and missed all my flights! 'It is Easter and all the legs of your journey are overbooked. You can probably get from here to Chicago, but you may then have to wait three days for a connection to England,' she told me. I looked at my husband who, I have to say at this point, was gasping the air like a goldfish out of water and who, for one of the few times since I have know him, was at a loss for words! I looked at my daughter, who simply said, 'How could this happen?' and burst into tears. I won't dwell on who had booked the tickets, but I did find myself asking the same question: 'How could this happen?' 'Come home, mum,' Hannah said, 'and then set off again.' My holiday was so short it was not worth it and besides, by now a little voice inside me was saying, 'Set off and see!' I had set off once and so I would go ahead and just see.

We parted and I did get a seat on every leg of the journey. Once again God and Charles were working as a team! He rushed home and made lots of phone calls to try and ensure things would be sorted ahead of me. They were, but I did not know he was doing that, so as I arrived at each airport and approached the check-in desk to explain my dilemma, it was God and not Charles who was getting the glory when I found they had managed to squeeze me in somewhere! Looking back I know both deserved thanks, but one more than the other because only one had been responsible for the ticket booking! (Whoops, I wasn't going to tell you!)

Why have I recounted this incident? Not to show you that I did set off and see, on the contrary, I set off, but I did not see. I was feeling too stressed and closed into myself and intent on my mission to get to England, whatever. I never really saw, let alone talked to anyone on the journey, until I got to Heathrow and then only superficially because I was tired and was near the end of my journey. When it was time to come back again, I sensed God saying to me, 'OK. Last time you set off, this time I want you to set off and *see!*' And I did. I arrived at Heathrow with a great sense of expectation and excitement. The departure lounge was heaving with people and there were very few spare seats. 'Open your eyes and look.' And I did and then I saw her, a very sad looking young woman sitting alone with one empty seat next to her – I took it. I must have sat there for about twenty minutes while she kept wiping away her tears and I prayed and finally said, 'Do you have a long wait?' That little question led to another and another and for the next hour, before I had to leave to get my flight, she poured out her broken heart to me. She was so like the woman at the well. I was both deeply distressed and exhilarated because I had been able to sit with her, listen to her, hear her and tell her about the 'man of understanding' who she so wanted to meet because she wanted 'more than religion'. We exchanged e-mail addresses as we parted, but we had already made the most important exchange – his offer of life in exchange for her life story. I had been too self-absorbed to see anyone on my outgoing journey, maybe there wasn't anyone there, but thank God he didn't disqualify me and I got another chance on the way home. What a gracious God have I!

As we look just one last time at the whole 'Set off and see' principle, I want to end with the place where for me it all started and God taught me through Scripture and life's circumstances what a fundamental and freeing lesson this was.

Several years ago I went through a period in my life when I felt what I can only describe as troubled in my spirit. I was restless and in turmoil deep within my heart. During that time God spoke to me through two complete strangers and they both said the same thing. One was a young German mother who I met in transit between Germany and Papua New Guinea. She and her husband had just sold their house, put the contents in storage and were now on their way to be missionaries in that fascinating, far-off land. I asked her about the family, their schooling, all the practical things that a mother's mind immediately thinks of. She could not answer all my questions; she didn't need to. This family was totally confident that the God who was sending them would be with them as they set off into the unknown. 'It's not enough to believe,' she said, 'you have to trust.'

Several days later, I was sitting in a small group at Capernwray Hall, a Bible College in the North of England, where we lived at the time, half listening to a young man from Eastern Europe who was sharing his thoughts on what was going on in his life at the time. His accent was rather thick and I had other things on my mind, but I was thinking how brave he was to be sharing such personal thoughts with a group of strangers and in a foreign language and then I heard it, clear as a bell, that same phrase, 'It's not enough to believe, you have got to trust.' I had got the message! I went and wrote that one potentially life-changing truth in my notebook and continued on in my turmoil, knowing the words were true, but at this point they were not true for me.

Sitting beside a stream, up in the mountains, a few weeks later, I blurted out all my anguish to a friend, finally admitting that my deepest fear and the one that was clouding everything else in my life at that point, was my husband's health. Medically there was no reason to think there was a problem, but in my heart I sensed one and I could keep it to myself no longer. She listened and prayed and I went home and wrote my husband a letter in which I poured out my fear and escalating anxiety. At last I had pin-pointed my deepest concern and I admitted it to him writing, 'I think you will have a heart attack and maybe it doesn't have to happen.' He was kind and gentle in his response, put the letter in his suitcase and went to Canada for two weeks ministry.

One week later, on a lovely summer evening in June, the phone rang and as I picked it up I heard words that would change our lives for ever, 'Hilary,' the voice said. 'This is John in Canada.' I felt as though I was suddenly suspended in a bubble of silence as I waited for the inevitable, and then it came, 'Charles is in hospital. He has had a very serious heart attack, but he is still alive.' My legs turned to jelly and my stomach plummeted, but my mind held fast as I asked questions and began to absorb the facts that were coming down the line. He had been out walking. He was miles from anywhere when a truck passed by and finding him sitting on a rock in pain had taken him to the nurses' station. He was now in intensive care. Would I like to speak to the cardiologist? More facts. Medical details. This was a massive heart attack. Charles may not live.

I put the phone down and realised I had to make decisions and make them quickly. I did not wake my son Matthew but brought the girls, Hannah and Laura into the kitchen and, as gently and as clearly as I could, explained the situation to them. They cried and begged me to reassure them that Dad would not die. I could not. 'I do not know,' I said. 'All I know is that God loves us. Do you believe that?' They could not answer immediately, but soon through their sobbing they both bravely said, 'Yes.' 'Then we can trust him,' I said. 'Whatever happens we can trust him. I am not going to pretend to you. If I promised you things that did not turn out to be true, you would never believe me again. I don't know what will happen, but God does and we can trust him, so go and start packing, we are going to Canada.'

I made many phone calls and in the midst of all the organising, which had forced me into automatic pilot mode, one of the girls came back into the kitchen. She had been having a talk with God in her room. 'It's going to be OK. I know,' she said. So strong and so sure, she gave me great strength. Now I knew the power of God's presence and the truth of his words so painfully planted in my heart a few weeks before: 'It's not enough to believe, you've got to trust.' I was being forced to 'Set off and see' and what amazing things I saw!

Within the next few hours and days God worked his miracles and I watched in awe! He had gone ahead of us every step of the way. The next morning we had four seats together on a plane, which otherwise was completely full. A Christian flight attendant came to comfort me, during the flight, having noticed how tired I looked. Charles was in the care of one of Toronto's best cardiologists, who had been a friend since childhood. One of my closest friends, in the world, was waiting for me as we got off the plane. We were loved and cared for and helped financially during that long summer in Toronto as we waited for and watched Charles' gradual recovery. God's presence was so real as we stepped into the scenario he had been preparing me for for months. One of the first things Charles said to me, when we arrived to find him hanging on to life by a thread and by all the tubes and monitors he was hooked up to, was, 'Are you mad with me?' I could only laugh as I cried!

I would not have chosen this path, but what a precious, painful journey it has been. I set off with fear and trepidation. I had no choice. I set off and I saw God – his love, his care, his tenderness, his complete trustworthiness as we put our trust in him. Each day is still an unknown. We did not know that Charles had had heart disease for many years and his heart will therefore always cause concern; each day is just one more opportunity to trust God.

One day I discovered a little group of women who, two thousand years ago, set off on the same journey and discovered the same God doing the most extraordinary things. Their story is found in Mark 16. After their wonderful Jesus had been crucified and buried, they set off expecting to find death, just as I did in my darkest thoughts, but, like me, they found life.

> When the Sabbath was over, Mary Magdelene, Mary the mother of James, and Salome bought spices so that they might go and anoint Jesus' body. Very early on the first day of the week, just after sunrise, they were on their way to the tomb and they asked each other, 'Who will roll the stone away from the entrance of the tomb?'
>
> But when they looked up, they saw that the stone, which was very large, had been rolled away. As they entered the tomb, they saw a young man dressed in a white robe sitting on the right side, and they were alarmed.
>
> 'Don't be alarmed,' he said. 'You are looking for Jesus the Nazarene, who was crucified. He has risen! He is not here' (Mk. 16:1–6).

What is so amazing about these women is that they set off with spices to anoint a body, behind a boulder, which was far too heavy for them to move. They could have stayed at home and reasoned this was an impossible mission and it was not worth setting off. But they didn't. They set off, driven by love, asking, 'Who will roll away the stone?' but failing to come up with a reasonable answer. What an adventure! What an opportunity for God to do the impossible and blow aside all their practical reservations. Doubts are no reason not to set off! Take them with you and maybe God will send an angel to silence them! Not only is he ahead of you every step of the way, he is also with you every step of the way, so what are you waiting for?

When I started writing this book I lived in England. During its writing (somewhere between about Chapters 5 and 6!) we moved to Canada. God called us to a wonderful church in Toronto, which just happened to be near Charles' cardiologist and of course my good friend. Although it was very clear that we should come and has been for many years (that's another story!) that does not mean it has been easy. Humanly there were many situations and people which could have held us back and prevented us setting off, but we all believe, in our family, that life is an adventure and it was a unanimous decision that we would just 'Set off and see.' We are still in the early days, but there are already many encouragements that God has allowed us to see and we are trusting him that there will be many more.

One Samaritan woman turned a whole town towards Jesus simply because she put down her pot, set off with the living water and gave it away. She did not understand everything, she did not need to. She had got a life and she could not keep it (him) to herself. The days of hiding in the dull, daily routine of existence were over; the adventure was beginning as she stepped into an ancient promise of God which still holds true:

No eye has seen,
No ear has heard,
no mind has conceived
what God as prepared for those who love him (Is. 64:4).

Are you willing to take that first tentative step out of the shadows, where you may have lived for so long?

'In him was life, and that life was the light of men. The light shines in the darkness, but the darkness has not understood it' (Jn. 1:4–5). The woman of Samaria did not understand everything. She still stammered in awe, 'Could this be . . . ? as she stepped out of the shadows. With her eyes still adjusting to the brilliance of his presence, she set off and made that first move to trust him. She had seen and heard enough to know he was the truth, he was the Messiah, he had found her and he had rescued her.

'He who has the Son has life; he who does not have the Son of God does not have life' (1 Jn. 5:12). For the first time in her weary existence, she had got a life. It's that simple. It's our choice. You want to get a life: simply believe, receive and then hang on for the most amazing adventure which, thanks to Jesus, will go on for ever! You're not sure who he is yet . . . come sit by this well, if you've got half an hour we could talk a while. You tell me your story and then, if you like, I'll tell you mine. Just put your pot down, you can always fill it later, it's not going anywhere. What's that you say, 'Neither are you?' Ever felt like you are stuck in a rut? . . .

The end

or

The beginning

(It's up to you!)

Meet the Man of Understanding

If what you have read in this book has lead you to the point where you would like to meet Jesus for yourself, then it is very simple – he is only a prayer away.

If you do not understand everything about him you may feel you are not ready. Maybe reading the rest of John's Gospel would answer many of your questions.

You are ready when you are willing to be real.

If you are willing to be real, then pray this prayer, quietly on your own:

Lord Jesus. I have never met you before but now I want to. I believe you made me. I believe you died on the cross for me and that through your death all my sin is forgiven. I believe you rose from the dead and sent your Holy Spirit to live in each of us when we open our lives to you. I know you have known me and patiently waited for me all my life. Thank you for waiting. Thank you for not giving up on me. Please forgive me for excluding you from my life. Now I ask you by your Holy Spirit to fill my life and to be my life forever. I want to know you more and I trust you, the Man of Understanding, to lead and guide me wherever you want me to go. Thank you. From now on we go together. Amen.

Tell someone you have come to know Jesus.

Find others who know and love him and meet with them.

Contact me if I can be of any help to you:

Hilary Price
The Peoples Church
374 Sheppard Avenue East
Willowdale
Ontario M2N 3B6
Canada.

Notes

[1] See interesting details about the role of women in Jewish society in *Marshalls Bible Handbook* (London: Marshall, Morgan and Scott, 1980).

[2] L. Morris, *The Gospel According to John* (Grand Rapids, MI: William B. Eerdmans Publishing Co., 1971), p. 259n.

[3] Ibid.

[4] Richard Morris, 'In Britain, it's always all our yesterdays', *The Times*, 24 June 2000.

[5] Henri Nouwen, *Sabbatical Journey* (New York: The Crossroad Publishing Company, 1998).

[6] Selwyn Hughes and Trevor J. Partridge, *Cover to Cover* (Farnham: CWR, 1999), p. 28.

[7] M. R. Vincent, *Word Studies in the New Testament*, Vol. 1 (Mac Dill, FL: MacDonald Publishing, n.d.), p. 428.

[8] Brennan Manning, *The Lion and the Lamb* (Grand Rapids, MI: Chosen Books, 1986).

[9] *Finding God* (Carlisle: Alpha, 2000), pp. 190–2.

[10] Larry Crabb. *Finding God* (Carlisle: Alpha, 2000), p. 181.

[11] The seed thought for this idea came from a talk by Jill Briscoe.

[12] William MacDonald, *Believers Bible Commentary* (Nashville, TN: Thomas Nelson Publishers, 1995), p. 1487.

[13] Victor Alfsen, *Realized but Unrecognized Eschaton* (www.cin.org.cin/fun/v8n12; accessed 21 January 1998).

[14] F.B. Meyer, *Elijah: and the Secret of his Power* (London: Morgan and Scott, n.d.).